The Magic of
CIRCLEWORK

About *The Magic of Circlework*

"*The Magic of Circlework* is a wonderful, right and useful book, essential for building and sustaining synergistic spiritual community. Read it and use it!"

—Andrew Harvey, author of *The Hope: A Guide to Sacred Activism*

"Circlework dissolves our separateness and awakens us to the shared heartspace that is our evolutionary potential. A deeply wise, compassionate and invaluable guide for our times."

—Tara Brach, author of *Radical Acceptance* and *True Refuge*

THE MAGIC OF CIRCLEWORK

The Practice Women Around the World
Are Using to Heal and Empower Themselves

JALAJA BONHEIM, PhD

The Magic of Circlework

Cover photo by Jari Poulin
Author photo by Elaine Derby

ISBN: 978-0-9993425-2-7
Circlework® is a registered trademark that refers exclusively to the work of Jalaja Bonheim and may not be used without her explicit consent.

To access your free bonus materials, go to **www.magicofcirclework.com** and use the temporary password **circlemagic**.

Meetings in Sacred Space
PO Box 848
Ithaca, NY 14851
www.jalajabonheim.com

DEDICATION

To all our ancestors, with gratitude.

CONTENTS

INTRODUCTION

Everything I see, hear, touch, feel, taste, speak, think, imagine, is completing a perfect circle God has drawn.

Meister Eckhart, 13th century

Ask me to list the benefits of Circlework, and I hardly know where to start—there are so many. But the one that comes to mind first is, without doubt, *connection*. Circlework is nothing if not a practice that connects us deeply—with others, with ourselves, and with Spirit.

Most people would agree that connection is a basic human need. Yet these days, it can be hard to come by. Vivek Murthy, who was the US Surgeon General from 2014 to 2017, has been sounding the alarm. "Loneliness," he writes, is a growing health epidemic. We live in the most technologically connected age in the history of civilization, yet rates of loneliness have doubled since the 1980s. Today, over 40 percent of adults in America report feeling lonely, and research suggests that the real number may well be higher."

As a physician, Murthy is keenly aware of the devastating effects this is having on our health:

> During my years caring for patients, the most common pathology I saw was not heart disease or diabetes; it was loneliness.... Loneliness and weak social connections are associated with a reduction in lifespan similar to that caused by smoking 15 cigarettes a day and even greater than that associated with

obesity. . . . Loneliness is also associated with a greater risk of cardiovascular disease, dementia, depression, and anxiety. . . . For our health and our work, it is imperative that we address the loneliness epidemic quickly.[1]

In part, this epidemic relates to the radical changes in family structures we've witnessed in recent decades. In 1970, 17 percent of US households were comprised of a single person. Back then, this was considered a shocking number, yet today, it has jumped to 28 percent. Thirty-five million Americans now live alone.

Yet simply widening our social circle is not the solution. After all, we all experienced what it's like to be surrounded by people yet feel profoundly lonely, invisible and isolated. Ultimately, what matters far more than the quantity of our social connections is their quality. Do our relationships have the intimacy, depth, and authenticity we crave? That is the real question.

For many people, the answer is no. Many of the participants in my circles say that for much of their life, they felt starved for intimacy—not sexual intimacy, but that sense of deep connectedness that links heart to heart and soul to soul. And yet, most of them aren't lonely, in the obvious ways. They have family, friends and community—and yet . . .

When they first discover Circlework, they're often amazed. "I never knew there was a place like this," they say. By which they mean, a place that feels both utterly safe and profoundly sacred. A place where they can come out of hiding and receive the deep nourishment that only true connection can provide.

It's sad to think that in our society, such places are so rare that many people despair of ever finding them. It doesn't have to be this way. Together, we have the power to initiate change, so that future generations won't have to suffer the same kind of loneliness that many take for granted today.

If you dream of experiencing deeper intimacy, authenticity, connection and love, not just with a single individual but with an entire community, I want to assure you that what you long for is indeed possible. It is not just a romantic vision or a utopian fantasy. On the contrary, it's your birthright—a birthright that Circlework is dedicated to helping you reclaim. Here, a woman called Lisette talks about this:

> Circlework is life-altering. It's completely outside of any experience I've ever had. It provides a deep kind of nourishment by breaking through the isolation so many people experience in our society. It quenches a longing for connection that so many people feel but that's really hard to find in our world.
>
> I believe we have to experience this connection in order to really know what we're looking for. If we don't get a chance to experience and practice how to come together in this very loving and compassionate and also extremely real way, we can't expect to know how to do that in the larger world.
>
> I personally needed to be in the circle long enough to really believe there really was another option. It's hard to envision this possibility and see it as part of our future when you haven't experienced it. The circle has given me that experience, the experience of a true alternative, and out of that, hope has come.

I, too, find that Circlework gives me hope. Whenever I'm overcome with despair for our crazy world, it restores my faith by showing me the extraordinary potential that lies within us all. More times than I can say, I've been awed by the powerful presence of the sacred that arises in our circles and by the profound encounters that occur. Surely no cathedral can match the beauty of a love-infused circle! Here, we feel the nearness and presence of Spirit and catch glimpses of the sacred feminine as she gazes through the eyes of each woman. Yet in this process, religion plays no part—there are no beliefs to adopt or dogmas to embrace.

I personally feel called to work primarily with women. I love creating opportunities, only too rare in our world, for women to rediscover the true meaning of sisterhood. I believe everyone benefits when women know their worth and have a strong voice. That said, I view Circlework as a practice, not just for women but for all humans. Men need circles just as much as women do—perhaps more so. I've seen how much they benefit from Circlework, and look forward to the day when every community has fabulous circles for men and women alike.

We usually join groups in hopes of feeling better, however we define that—more peaceful, perhaps, or more centered, skilled, or confident. But for many of the women I work with, that isn't enough. Of course they too want to feel good—who doesn't? But they are also acutely aware of the suffering that surrounds them and the perils our world is facing. Many are mothers who are worried about the future of their children. And so, they are asking themselves: How can I make a difference? How can I be a force for healing in this world? How can I be of service? They want to lead meaningful, fulfilling lives, but they also want to help create a more peaceful world for future generations. In Circlework, they find a tool that helps them walk their path in balance and joy.

My Healing Journey

I've been training circle leaders for over three decades now. But when did I myself first experience the healing power of the circle? As I consider this question, I remember an experience I had over forty years ago, in my early twenties.

I had joined an ongoing therapy group for men and women. Like most therapy groups, we too sat in a circle. However, the significance of the circle was never mentioned, nor did we give any conscious thought to the form we were using. Still, in hindsight, I see how essential the presence of the circle was to the healing I received there.

To create spaces that are safe, sacred, and conducive to healing, we need not gather in a circle. But for reasons that will become obvious throughout this book, circle gatherings are ideally suited to the task. Just as a good hammer makes a carpenter's job much easier, the circle is a tool perfectly suited to the creation of sacred space.

At the time, I was experimenting with many different therapeutic modalities. Keenly aware of my own woundedness, I felt like the real me was hidden most of the time. Like many young people, I was both intensely social and profoundly lonely. Shy and insecure, I longed to break free in the worst way. Yet at the same time, I was terrified of showing up authentically.

But why did I feel the need to hide my true self? When I asked myself that question, a very small, scared voice replied, "Because I don't trust people." I knew this voice had a lot of power over me. And while it claimed to protect me, I could see it was keeping me isolated and alone.

So one evening, I arrived at our therapy group determined to speak honestly about my fears. It wasn't easy—I longed to bolt out the door, never to be seen again. Overwhelmed with shame, I avoided looking anyone in the eye. But I had made a commitment to myself that I was determined to keep. And so, I stayed, and I spoke.

When I was finished, the therapist asked whether he might lead me on a little inner journey. "Sure," I said.

I no longer recall his words, only that somehow, he helped me explore the source of my fears. Like many children, I'd spent several painful years as an outcast in school. Yet this, I now realized, was merely the tip of a major iceberg. Images began welling up of cruelty and violence that weren't sourced in my personal experience. Rather, they reflected the trauma of growing up as a Jew in postwar Germany. Children are like sponges, and I had absorbed all kinds of horrific images and stories that I had no way of processing. And so, without even realizing it, I had lost all trust in my own kind.

"How about us?" my therapist asked gently. Weeping, unable to speak, I buried my face in my hands and shook my head. No, I didn't trust them, either. I didn't trust anyone.

If you had asked me prior to this evening whether I felt connected to the members of my therapy group, I would have said yes, I did. But now, I discovered that at the deepest level, the answer was no. After all, connection requires trust, and in that regard, I was sorely lacking.

But when I realized that my distrust included this gathering of people from whom I had experienced nothing but kindness, I thought: "This is an intolerable way to live." There and then, I resolved to find out who my fellow humans really were. I took a deep breath.

Tear-streaked and terrified, I raised my head, turned to the group, and slowly looked them in the eye, one by one. The shutters of my heart were wide open, and I was allowing them to see me all the way to my core. But I also found I was seeing them in a new way, with greater clarity and without the interference of fear. This was the moment of turning. It was the moment of saying: "Yes, I am willing to see and be seen." Instead of running away, I was, for the first time, opting to show up. Instead of choosing the apparent safety of isolation and withdrawal, I was choosing intimacy and connection.

What I understand now—though I didn't then—is that our psyche perceives any circle of human beings (and as I mentioned, my therapy group was a circle of sorts) as a microcosm of the entire species. The power of the circle is such that even a small circle evokes the totality of the human community. So, as I turned to face the circle, I was taking a new look, not just at these individuals, but at my entire species.

What I saw, as I looked at these men and women, was that they were fully present: they were truly paying attention, truly interested. Instead of disdain or disgust, I saw caring and—yes—love. Some were crying. More than anything else, it was their evident compassion that broke down my defenses. I began to sob, and continued to grieve for weeks, not just for the pain I was carrying, but for the shame that had caused me to wall off my feelings, and for the terrible isolation in which I had lived in for so many years. And so, I began to heal my wounded relationship to the human race.

The Evolution of Circlework

It would be another decade before I myself would start leading circles. First, I had a lot more healing and growth to do, both in Europe and in

India, where I lived for several years, studying temple dance, meditation and Hindu philosophy.

By the time I came to the United States, the early 1980s had arrived. People—especially women—were hungry for new ways of gathering in community and exploring their inner life.

I too was filled with longing. Looking to the past, I saw the temples of the Indian priestesses whose ways I'd been studying. What, I wondered, might such temple spaces look like today? I imagined a place where women would tell stories, laugh and cry together, and feel deeply nourished by the authenticity of their connections.

My Western education had taught me how to communicate through words and how to facilitate the exchange of ideas and information. India, on the other hand, had taught me about those deeper levels of connection that require us to be present, not so much in our minds as in our hearts and bodies.

I knew nothing about circle leadership, at least not on a conscious level. What I did know, however, is that the key to feeling connected is open-heartedness. Also, I knew how often we use words to shield rather than uncover the heart. Talking, therefore, would not be enough. Rather, I wanted the process to include beautiful music, ritual, silence, touch and immersion in nature. Within a society addicted to incessant thinking, I wanted us to co-create a sanctuary where we could transcend our mind.

When you find yourself yearning for something that doesn't seem to exist, you have two options—give up, or attempt to manifest your dreams. I chose the latter. Since I couldn't find the kind of space I envisioned, I resolved to try and create it.

Thus, Circlework was born. My first circles had a much stronger focus on movement and dance than they currently do. Yet from the very start, all seven pillars of Circlework, as outlined on page 26, were present. I soon discovered how much I loved this work, and that many other women shared my yearning for a new kind of temple space.

The Work Grows

After I'd been leading circles for a few years, women started asking for training, so that they might share the process of Circlework with others. So in the 1990s, I began training groups of women.

It quickly became clear that many women who had the desire and capacity to bring the gifts of Circlework to their communities would be unable to afford the training without financial assistance. So in 2001, I founded the Institute for Circlework, a non-profit organization based in Ithaca, NY. Since its inception, the Institute for Circlework has provided scholarships to hundreds of trainees and has supported the evolution and practice of Circlework around the world.

Today, graduates of the Circlework Leadership Training are facilitating circles throughout North America, but also in India and Afghanistan, Kenya and Australia, Israel and Palestine, Germany, Italy and other countries. They include women from all walks of life—social workers, activists, corporate executives, religious leaders, therapists, counselors and health care workers. You can find them in schools and colleges, hospitals and prisons, community centers and corporations.

How Women are Using Circlework

◎ I lead a monthly circle for women business leaders and a monthly circle for women presidents.

◎ I lead two circles. One is a women's support circle. The second focuses specifically on sexuality. The women describe the circle as a haven. A few who have moved away in the course of the last years have told me that this is the thing they miss the most.

◎ I lead a circle for parents of kids who have learning disabilities of various kinds and are having a hard time in the mainstream schools.

◎ I'm a minister. I do all of my small group work in circles. I'm also moving towards bringing circle dances to our contemporary worship service.

◎ I lead circles in the corporate world. I always bring a candle, and we begin with silence. Afterwards, people always say, "Could we have this more often?" They really hunger for those moments of quiet.

◎ I lead women's spirituality circles. They've been very successful and I am planning to do more. I also want to start a bereavement circle soon.

◎ I co-lead a circle for corporate executives. I love seeing one woman at a time come into her wholeness. It's a joy to offer this work and a gift to be a part of it.

◎ I have taken Circlework into my work as a child protection worker. I just led a circle for a women's drug and alcohol recovery program and will be doing that every month. I'm also planning to lead circles for women escaping domestic violence.

◎ I am a physician and have been leading a circle for cancer patients. It's been the most amazing, humbling, awe-inspiring experience.

Taking it to the Middle East

Since 2005, I've been leading circles for Jewish and Palestinian women in the Middle East. Needless to say, the impact of violence, war and trauma on these women is immense. Sometimes, the grief and despair we are required to hold feels overwhelming. Yet ultimately, there is healing, hope, and an undeniable sense of holiness.

Working in the Middle East opened my eyes to the truly revolutionary power of connection. I already knew, thanks to my circles in the United States, how essential connection is to our personal sense of well-being and happiness. But in Israel and Palestine, I realized that connection is also the key to improving relationships between entire groups and nations.

Unfortunately, most governmental responses to conflict, be it in the Middle East or elsewhere, are fear-based. As such, they naturally favor disconnection over connection. One of the most horrific results of this approach is the monstrosity of a wall that Israel has erected around the West Bank. The more fear, anger, hatred and mistrust we feel toward others, the more courage it takes to open to connection. It is easier—far easier—to build yet another wall or install yet another military checkpoint than to face the "others" with all the physical and emotional vulnerability this entails. Will they be willing to hear our pain? With they be able to empathize with us, or forgive us? There are no guarantees. And yet, I believe there is no other path to peace.

In my circles in the Middle East, we essentially do the same thing as in the United States: we connect. We listen deeply to ourselves and others, and we speak honestly and authentically, even when it's hard. Over and over, I've seen how this allows our relationships to transform. We begin to feel compassion and even love for people whom we formerly distrusted, feared or even hated. We begin to recognize peace as a very real possibility, and indeed as the only option that makes any practical sense. The barriers between us dissolve, and our oneness stands revealed, like the full moon emerging from billowing clouds.

Regardless of where a circle is held, the task of bringing down the walls that separate us is always the same. In my circles in the United States, the enmity between Jews and Palestinians is not our focus. Yet here, too, our circles tend to bring us face to face with people whom we might ordinarily not meet. The very young meet the very old. The wealthy meet the poor. White women connect with women of color. One by one, our prejudices crumble and the labels we have slapped on each other dissolve.

Circlework is for Women Who Want . . .

◎ To experience authentic sisterhood with other women;

◎ To engage in spiritual practices that have no religious or ideological baggage;

◎ To be empowered and empower other women;

◎ To hone their skills in maintaining happy, harmonious relationships;

◎ To cultivate qualities such as gentleness, receptivity, compassion, and courage—all keys to maintaining harmonious relationships;

◎ To honor the physical body as a piece of Mother Earth, ancient and wise, vulnerable and sacred, flawed yet deserving of love;

◎ To serve the greater planetary community.

Embodying the Mandala

Personally, I've never viewed the circle as a mere geometric form. From the start, I perceived it as a living field of presence and consciousness, as a friend, an ally and a sacred being. Often, I think of it as an angel who has, since the beginning of time, been showing us how we might live in harmony with all beings. In my eyes, the circle is a great spiritual teacher who can show us how to make our relationships sweet and joyful, how to deal with obstacles, and how to find our way through the fog of our ego into the clear light of love.

In my reverence for circles, I am by no means alone. From the dawning of human history, our ancestors have been fascinated with them and fully aware of their numinous power. Most religious traditions hold the circle sacred as an expression of divine perfection. And on every continent, all the most ancient examples of human art are circles. In a cave in India, for example, archeologists recently discovered a cupule—a circular hollow carved into rock—estimated to be between 200,000 and 790,000 years old. Clearly, we've been in love with circles for a very long time.

These days, many people see the circle merely as a convenient format for group gatherings. They might praise its egalitarian spirit—everyone sits at equal distance from the center—but that's about as far as it goes. In contrast, Circlework invites us to actually *embody* the mandala.

Mandala is a Sanskrit word usually translated as "sacred circle." But what exactly does that mean? It's a question we'll return to at a later point. For now, let me just say that a mandala is an expression of wholeness, centeredness, balance and sacredness. In India, there is a saying, "What you meditate upon, that you become." I believe this is true. By meditating on the circle, we too become more centered, balanced and whole.

Another important point to understand is that the language by which the mandala communicates is known as sacred geometry, and that sacred geometry is an essential aspect of Circlework. Through its skillful use, we constellate the mandala, not only within our circles, but above all within our own consciousness. When we leave the circle, the mandala goes with us as a vortex of healing presence that continues to anchor us in goodness, wholeness and holiness.

Previously I mentioned some of the attributes of the mandala, such as centeredness, balance and sacredness. I think you'll agree that these are qualities worth cultivating in ourselves and our world. But the foremost attribute of the mandala, as well as its greatest gift, is oneness.

We all want to feel at one with ourselves, our loved ones and our world. Yet the sad reality is that in our day and age, our communities are hopelessly fractured and fragmented. Under these conditions, oneness isn't just a lofty spiritual goal. Rather, it's a key to our survival and arguably our greatest need at this point in time. Unless we can realize our basic oneness, we have no chance of overcoming global challenges such as climate change.

A circle is, of course, a universal symbol of oneness. A mandala, on the other hand, is no mere symbol. Rather, it's a sacred tool or a medicine. When we're feeling fragmented or separate, it can evoke in us the experience of connection, unity and oneness. Like a bridge, it can lead us from discord to harmony and from isolation to connection. Circlework is a way of consciously and intentionally applying mandala medicine so that we might awaken to our oneness, both as a circle and as a global family.

In our society, most people don't think of the circle as a medicine. Nonetheless our collective consciousness seems to recognize its healing power. Labyrinths are springing up in people's back yards, book stores are carrying stacks of mandala coloring books, and hordes of tourists are flocking to ancient stone circles found around the world. It's surely no coincidence that at a time when we urgently need to realize our oneness as a planetary family, all sorts of mandala-based practices have become immensely popular.

If the stories you're about to read whet your appetite to experience Circlework for yourself, wonderful. But the bottom line is that what works in the circle also works in life. Apply the basic principles of Circlework, and you too will see your world becoming sweeter and more peaceful, your relationships deeper and more fulfilling. Simply reading this book will begin to awaken the mandala within you. And once that inner mandala has been constellated, it will accompany you wherever you go, helping you stay more balanced and centered, peaceful and whole. You'll know the circle then, not only as a magical healing tool, but also as an inner resource that you can call upon at any time.

Learning the Art of Circle Facilitation

This book will introduce you to Circlework as a spiritual practice that is uniting women around the planet, and that can help you too discover a new sense of wholeness. Interwoven into the fabric of this book are the voices of hundreds of women who have participated in my circles and trainings. Their words will help you better understand the magic that we can work together, but also the challenges we face.

What this book *won't* do is teach you to facilitate circles.

If you're looking for "how to" guidelines, consider purchasing the Circlework Training Manual, which covers every aspect of circle leadership. Though originally written for participants of the Circlework Leadership Training, the Manual is also available to the general public. It covers the practical details of how to set up circles and how to deal with the challenges that arise. It includes exercises, meditations, transcripts, frequently asked questions, and much more. Under "Resources," you'll find information on how to order the *Circlework Training Manual*.

Remember, however, that even the best manual can only take you so far. You can read books about swimming till the cows come home, but until you actually get in the water, you'll never learn to swim. In this context, getting in the water means actually participating in circles. Try out different ones. Find out what you like and don't like. Successful circles will help you discover what works. From the less successful ones, you'll learn what doesn't.

Get all the training you can. Initially, circle leadership might seem easy. Yet those who try to facilitate circles without adequate preparation often discover that it isn't as easy as they imagined. The circle is a simple form, but the human psyche is not. I've heard plenty of stories about circles that fell apart or ended in disaster. Many a circle has found an untimely end due to a lack of skilled facilitation.

Of course, there are those who believe that a circle shouldn't have a designated leader at all. Leadership, they say, implies a hierarchy that is incompatible with the egalitarian spirit of the circle.

In my view, this is a misunderstanding. Yes, the circle is a non-hierarchical form; we all sit at equal distance from the center. However, the absence or presence of hierarchy in a circle does not correlate to the absence or presence of a designated leader. Leaderless circles often develop distinct power structures. Certain individuals take on certain roles, and while there may be no stated hierarchy, it exists nonetheless.

Vice versa, the presence of a leader does not imply that one person has been elevated above others. In Circlework, leadership is merely viewed as a role, never as a mark of personal superiority. Just as an airplane needs a pilot, a circle may benefit from having one or several facilitators. These are, however, no more superior to other members of the circle than pilots are to their passengers.

Each circle is different and unique. The important question, therefore, is: What structure would best serve the needs of this particular circle? Some will do just fine without a leader. Others will benefit immensely from good facilitation. If you want a place where you feel totally safe, there's nothing like working with a trusted, experienced leader. This is especially true when conflict or explosive emotions are at play. For example, the women I work with in the Middle East need skilled leaders who can help them create a safe container for the deep work they are doing.

These days, ministers, counselors and therapists are often expected to lead circles without having received any specialized training. Often, they end up feeling frustrated and stressed. This is not a sign of personal failure. Rather, it highlights our collective state of ignorance in regards to circle facilitation. Even among those well-versed in matters of psychology, spirituality, and personal growth, there's a striking lack of knowledge about how circles function and how to make them safe.

The circle is a powerful tool, and learning to use it well takes time, practice, and dedication. Yet the rewards are tremendous. Granted, I am biased. But as I see it, the circle is a tool we urgently need—today, more than ever. Ancient though it is, it is perfectly suited to helping us tackle many of our current challenges, from social isolation to prejudice and racism.

So allow me now to introduce you to my beloved friend, teacher

THE SEVEN PILLARS
OF CIRCLEWORK

In unison, these seven elements make Circlework the uniquely powerful, transformative experience that it is.

1 **Planetary Consciousness:** Circlework recognizes the oneness and interconnectedness of the global community. We are not working in isolation, but as part of a greater web of planetary healers. Interconnected as we are at every level, from the physical to the spiritual, we dedicate our work to our own personal healing and to that of the entire planetary community.

2 **Spirituality:** Spirituality, defined as opening to the knowledge of our oneness with others and the cosmos, is an essential human need. Yet in our world, it all too often goes unmet. Many no longer follow a religious path. Others find that their religious practice does not give them the soul nourishment they crave. Circlework provides a range of opportunities for participants to access Spirit in ways that transcend religion and are not based on any particular ideology or belief system. Immersed in sacred space, they rediscover their own authentic spirituality and are encouraged to live in alignment with their soul's deepest desires.

3 **The Mandala:** Circlework approaches the geometric form of the circle as a medicine that can help us become what it is: whole, centered, balanced and sacred. In this respect, Circlework stands

in the lineage of all those throughout the ages who saw the circle as a form imbued with sacred power, capable of healing body, mind and soul. Circlework also builds on the insights of C.G. Jung, who described the circle as an archetypal image that lies within the psyche of every human being and can help us realize our wholeness and divinity. By maintaining a constant focus on sacred geometry, Circlework awakens participants to the circle as an inner source of wisdom and guidance. The presence of the center, universally equated with the divine Source, allows them to co-create sacred space, without resorting to religious terminology or dogma.

4 The Feminine: On the one hand, Circlework empowers women by helping them experience their beauty and value and by giving them opportunities, only too rare in our world, to rediscover the true meaning of sisterhood. On the other hand, Circlework also fosters qualities that our society associates with the feminine and marginalizes, such gentleness, tenderness, compassion, softness, beauty and grace. At this time in history, it's essential that both men and women cultivate these supposedly "feminine" (though actually universal) qualities, since they hold the key to maintaining peaceful, fulfilling relationships between individuals, groups and nations.

5 Embodiment: One of the aims of Circlework is to help people transition from head- to heart-thinking, two concepts I discuss at length in my book *The Sacred Ego*. To achieve this shift, we need to move the center of our attention from our head into our body. Circlework includes a wide range of practices designed to facilitate this shift. These practices give the experience a unique flavor. Whereas most other types of circle gatherings mainly involve sitting and talking, Circlework includes movement, touch, sounding, silence and immersion in nature. As participants come home to their bodies, they also come home to the earth.

6 Relational Education: As one glance at the evening news can remind us, our species is currently facing massive challenges in the arena of interpersonal relationships. We urgently need what I call "relational education"—the kind that enables us to maintain peaceful, harmonious relationships. By providing it, Circlework prepares us to relate peacefully to diverse kinds of people, including those whose beliefs and views differ significantly from our own. It empowers us to stay centered, spacious and open, even in the midst of challenging interactions—a crucial key to maintaining peace, be it between individuals, groups or nations.

7 Spaciousness: Our society is overwhelmingly busy, noisy and crowded, and our minds tend to match the frantic pace of our outer environment. Circlework is decidedly countercultural in its emphasis on spaciousness as an essential key to happiness and spiritual fulfillment. Through guided meditations and other practices, it helps us access the inner sense of freedom and expansiveness we long for. As much as possible, retreats and trainings are held in spacious natural environments and include a lot of "down" time.

THE SEVEN NEEDS

As tribal circles evolved to address the needs of tribal peoples, so Circlework is designed to address our present needs. These are the seven main ones we focus on:

1 The Need to Bridge our Differences

Skillfully facilitated circles can bring us together in ways that reveal our common humanity. They can help diverse groups of people—including those divided by conflict, war, hatred and distrust—find healing and reconciliation. As I mentioned previously, I myself lead circles in the Middle East, both in Israel and the West Bank. Of course, exposing oneself to diversity of any kind can be challenging. At the same time, it's part of what makes Circlework so powerful and exciting. How else shall we mend the fault lines that are devastating our communities and our world? By shifting our focus from our differences to our common humanity, we build a foundation for peace.

2 The Need for Connection and Intimacy

We are currently witnessing an epidemic of loneliness. Vast numbers of people no longer experience the closeness and connection they need. This state of chronic deprivation leaves them vulnerable to all sorts of problems, from drug and alcohol addiction to depression and violence. Circles can connect us in ways that feel intimate and meaningful, but also comfortable and safe.

3   The Need for Community

Today, many traditional community structures have dissolved. At the same time, circles are increasingly serving as a kind of womb space where new forms of community are being gestated. Of course, not every circle has an long-term focus. But some do, and among them, many have been extremely successful and have endured not just for years but decades. Together, their members have been through marriages and divorces, joys and sorrows. Such people will readily tell you that they can no longer imagine life without their circle.

4   The Need to Shift from Head- to Heart-Thinking

We are, as a society, addicted to what I call "head-thinking" — thinking that splits the mind from the heart. Divisive as it is, head-thinking has always been a problematic habit. Yet now that we have entered the global era, it's become an unsustainable addiction that is endangering our future. Therefore Circlework consistently supports us in listening to our hearts, and using our mind in service of the heart. As we shift to heart-thinking, we find that our relationships become more harmonious and fulfilling. Heart-thinking helps us realize our oneness—not as an abstract concept, but as a felt, embodied truth. By committing to the practice of heart-thinking, we support a collective shift that can make the difference between war and peace, annihilation and survival.

5 The Need for Stress Relief

These times we live in are immensely stressful. Many are affected by war, poverty or displacement. Others might be struggling with job pressure, poor health, or relationship problems. One way or another, we're all swimming through a thick stew of insecurity and fear. Even if our personal lives are in great shape, one glance at the morning news is enough to make our blood pressure soar. We need support in staying centered, relaxed, and balanced. Circlework integrates a wide range of practices designed to foster inner peace. Movement and touch, for example, are prime tools for alleviating stress. Combine them with the centering medicine of the mandala, guided meditations, and supportive community, and you have an extremely effective form of stress relief.

6 The Need for Spiritual Nourishment

In the past, most people looked to religion to address their need for intimacy with Spirit. Yet today, religion alone is not enough—not, at least, if we identify as planetary citizens. Religion is, after all, an essentially tribal phenomenon. Every religion evolved out of a specific cultural context, in response to the needs of a specific people. Yet as planetary citizens, we need to be able to share sacred space with all kinds of people, including those whose beliefs differ from ours. Circles are the ideal tool for accomplishing this. Universally recognized as a sacred symbol, the circle can unite us in a sense of sacred presence that transcends all belief systems.

7 The Need to Transform Patriarchy

Patriarchy, especially in its post-industrial manifestations, is unsustainable. Regardless of whether we're male or female, it warps our consciousness, causing us to equate vulnerability with weakness and violence with strength. All societies governed by patriarchal values are riddled with violence. The situation is all the more dangerous considering that in the global era, war, too, tends to be a global phenomenon. The deployment of nuclear weapons—a possibility that patriarchy loves to flirt with—would guarantee a global catastrophe of unprecedented proportions. Circlework recognizes the inhumane and unsustainable nature of the values and beliefs that patriarchy instills in us, offering us the antidote of gentleness, compassion, humility and generosity.

CHAPTER 1

Entering the Sanctuary

*Step out of the circle of time
And into the circle of love.*

Rumi

Nestled amidst rolling hills, dark woods and shimmering ponds lies a large retreat center. Overhead, hawks circle lazily, their gilded wings glistening in the afternoon sun. A doe stands by the edge of the meadow, sniffing the air until, reassured that all is well, she returns to grazing.

In this oasis of serenity and peace, a group of women is about to converge for the Circlework Leadership Training. Cradled in beauty, they'll spend an entire week together—learning and growing, sharing laughter and tears, walks and meals, dreams and visions.

I've arrived early. Sitting on the deck, I close my eyes and think about the women who are about to arrive and the magic we're about to co-create. Each circle is different and unique. Each one has its own personality and its own work to accomplish. Each one poses special challenges.

I pray that our work together be of benefit to all beings, that each woman might receive what she needs, that our circle be a haven of love and peace, happiness and joy, healing and awakening. And that in a week's time, we leave not only with new insights and skills, but also with beloved new sisters.

Soon, the women begin to arrive. Most live in the United States. Several, however, have travelled thousands of miles to get here. Some have taken the Circlework Training many times and are seasoned circle leaders in their own right. Others, I'm meeting for the first time. One young woman tells me she's never participated in a women's circle of any kind. "But," she says, "I know I need to be here."

It's a statement I hear frequently. The circle can call a woman in many ways. Sometimes, her dreams tell her to come. Sometimes, she just knows intuitively that it's the right thing, even if she's never before experienced Circlework.

Once everyone has arrived, we gather for dinner over steaming, fragrant pots of food. Then, we convene in the large meeting space. Darkness has now fallen, and the green hills are shimmering under the soft light of the moon. Inside, candlelight casts a gentle glow on our faces.

The women settle down, some in chairs, others on the floor. A hush falls, and the immense silence of the night comes flooding in. In the distance, we hear the plaintive hooting of an owl.

Someone heaves a deep sigh.

"Welcome," I say.

VOICES FROM THE CIRCLE

I am crying tears of relief. It feels so good to be here again. I missed the circle so much. Once again, I feel awed by its power and privileged to be part of it.

To feel safe, the women need to understand the rules of the game. So, I list the ground rules of our circle: Keep confidential women's personal information. Come on time. Don't do what I say unless it feels right to you. Remember that you are here for the nourishment of your own soul. Listen to your needs. If at any point you feel uncomfortable, don't just leave. Talk to me or to another member of the circle.

I know the women are tired. I also know that what looks like tiredness is in part fear. As yet, nobody has spoken of it, but I can smell it in the air like a faint odor. For some, coming here is one of the scariest things they've ever done. "What's going to happen? Will I have a good time? Will I regret my decision?"

Later, a business owner called Lorna will speak of the terror that overcame her after she signed up, and how she tried to talk herself out of coming:

> This training is the thing I wanted to do most in the whole world. I've been looking forward to it for months. And yet, for the last two weeks it's been the thing I least wanted to do. I thought of every reason I could to back out. On the plane yesterday I kept thinking, why am I feeling this way? I'm normally not nervous about coming to groups. But there's something about this work that is different and feels very powerful. I'm happy to say that tonight, when I felt the energy of the circle and looked into everybody's eyes, my fear dissolved and I knew I wanted to be here.

I know that others share Lorna's fears. They too are attracted to Circlework because they're hungry for authentic, intimate connection. But to let themselves be seen unmasked, in their naked truth, is scary as hell. And whereas in a classroom, one can hide, in a circle, there is nowhere to hide, nothing to shield the soft, vulnerable front of one's body. Like it or not, one is visible.

I think back to a student of mine who once led a circle for homeless women. Initially, there was no way she could convince them to sit in a circle—they simply could not tolerate the exposure. A few brave ones would sit up front while everyone else hid behind them. It was a measure of the circle's success that, after eight weeks of weekly meetings, everyone spontaneously chose to sit in a true circle, visible and exposed. The process had given them the confidence and courage they needed to show up.

The Adversary

In theory, we long to immerse ourselves in sacred space. Yet as we approach that threshold, we may encounter unexpected inner resistance.

VOICES FROM THE CIRCLE

The circle is so simple, yet very mysterious. It evokes a spiritual presence that is very tangible yet also unfathomable and subtle. It guides me, moves me, calls me. It's available for all of us, and in that energy, that presence, we can unfold and grow.

The circle is where we want to be, we know that. Still, something holds us back, warns us not to proceed and pleads with us to turn back.

What is this strange force that seems to oppose the yearning of our soul and would prevent us from satiating our hunger for communion with Spirit?

It's been called some extremely negative names, such as Satan or the devil. Personally, I prefer to think of this inner force as the Adversary. The Adversary is like my personal trainer. It forces me to work harder and makes me stronger. It sits at the threshold to sacred space, much like the scary gargoyles that crouch over the entrance to medieval cathedrals, or like the monsters of Tibetan Buddhism iconography who guard the four entrances to the mandala. The adversary is, in other words, not a mistake, not an aberration. It's *supposed* to be there.

All this is to say, don't be surprised if, when standing on the threshold to sacred space, you experience a sudden surge of resistance. Let's say you've decided to meditate for half an hour every morning. You really want to do this, you know it will do you good, and you're actually looking forward to it. But when the time comes, the Adversary is right there. "No way," it says. "Not today. Maybe tomorrow." Then, it cites all sorts of perfectly rational reasons why right now, meditating is a really bad idea. You have too much to do. Guests are coming. Your back feels achy. Whatever.

In some people, the adversary is stronger than in others. For them, holding to any discipline can be a struggle. Even brushing their teeth in the morning can feel like a huge challenge.

"I need to connect with Spirit more than I need life itself," a woman recently told me. "And yet, I just don't let myself go there. I feel like I'm cursed or something."

But having a strong inner adversary is no curse. It simply means that you're called to be a warrior. By warrior, I don't mean someone who wages war, but someone who cultivates physical, emotional,

VOICES FROM THE CIRCLE

I'm already dancing on the edge of all my core issues, not just one but all of them. And we've just started! I can't believe how fast this is happening.

mental and spiritual strength. To enter sacred space, you need to become stronger than your inner adversary.

Telling that gargoyle to go away is useless. Instead, try to get to know it better. Observe it, the way an ornithologist might observe a rare bird, with patience, respect and curiosity. Don't judge yourself because you're experiencing resistance.

On the other, hand, resistance shouldn't automatically be dismissed or ignored, either. After all, it might be informing you that something just isn't right for you. So look carefully and ask, "What kind of resistance is this? Is this the voice of intuitive wisdom? Or is it the voice of the Adversary who wants to keep me safely enclosed in the realm of the ego? Is it the voice of love or of fear?"

As I look around the circle, I know that each woman has had to battle this inner adversary, each in her own way. And so, I inwardly salute the courage she has demonstrated, simply by showing up. She is here because her commitment to nurturing her heart and soul have won out over her fear.

VOICES FROM THE CIRCLE

When we were looking into each other's eyes, I thought, "This. This is how I want to live my life. I want to be able to meet people from this place of spacious intimacy all the time.

Time to Move

Having covered the ground rules, I ask the women to stand up and push back their seats. "Let's move!" I say.

Many aren't really present yet. Their bodies have arrived, but their thoughts are still on the road. Movement will help them let go of the past and open to the here and now. Plus, it's an extremely effective tool for shedding anxiety.

Of course I'm well aware that putting their bodies on display may be the last thing they want to do right now. Therefore I hasten to assure them that the plan is extremely simple: We're just going to shake out some of the tension in our bodies.

The music I play has a wild, primal beat.

"Close your eyes," I suggest.

Inviting women to close their eyes will alleviate self-consciousness and help them understand: this isn't about being observed or judged. Also, closing their eyes will make it easier to turn inward and feel whatever they're feeling.

First, I invite them to shake loose their hands and arms, legs and shoulders.

"Shake out your belly," I continue. "Shake out your face. Shake out your brain. You don't need it right now. In this moment, there is absolutely nothing you need to think about or figure out."

"Make space in your body for your breath," I continue. "Give yourself permission to breathe."

At some point, I invite them to add sounds to their movement. Grunts, groans and squeals begin to spin through the air.

All this commotion might seem quite pointless. Yet in fact, several important messages are being conveyed: "This is a place where you can have a voice. This is a place where you can make sounds that *aren't* pretty and controlled. This is a place where your animal body is welcome. This is a place where you can move any way you want to, and nobody is going to tell you you're doing it wrong. This is a place where you can stand quietly without doing anything at all, even if everyone else is dancing wildly. This is a place where you can be *you*."

Entering Sacred Space

As the drumming draws to a close, the silence of the night comes flooding in once again.

"Close your eyes," I say. "Place your hands on your heart, and welcome yourself into this moment. Welcome yourself with the same tenderness with which a mother would welcome her beloved child."

In the background, a woman with a voice like a nightingale is singing softly. Though her song has no words, the rawness of her yearning touches our hearts and coaxes them to open.

"I am your soul" she seems to be saying. "I've been waiting for you.

Voices from the Circle

I feel this quiet sense of homecoming and fullness. Here, I can really be.

Waiting, waiting, for so long. Listen. Pay attention to me, dear one."

I begin to guide the women into sacred space—space consecrated to the care of the soul. I remind them that the word "sacred" comes from the Latin *sacrare*, to set apart. Our circle is, in other words, a place that is set apart from the frenzy of daily life.

All sacred structures, from Westminster Abbey to the caves of Ajanta, help us feel that we have entered another world. The moment we step through the doors of a cathedral, mosque, synagogue or temple, we know we are not in a friend's living room. There might be high, arched doorways and stained glass windows, music and incense. There might be the sound of bells or gongs.

Yet all these trappings are useful only insofar as they facilitate an *inner* shift from a state of mental busyness into a quieter and more expansive frame of mind. In our circle, we are now making that very shift. However, instead of relying on sacred architecture, we're tapping the power of our shared intention.

For several minutes, I invite the women to connect with their hearts and souls. Speaking softly, I talk to them about the journey we are embarking on. Many still have their eyes closed; several faces are glistening with tears. This is good: It means they're starting to connect with themselves in a deeper way.

But is this really a safe place to share their hopes and longings? They're not sure yet. After all, many have only just met. To feel safe, they need to check each other out: Who are these strange women? Can they be trusted?

In any other environment, we'd all be talking right now. That is, after all, how people ordinarily scope others out and decide how they feel about them. They talk, and based on how the conversation goes, they invite them over for dinner—or not.

The problem is, while words can connect us, they can also *dis*-connect us from our hearts and keep us locked in our heads. If, right now, I encouraged the women to start talking, that is exactly what would happen. Instead of venturing into the mystery, they would stay

VOICES FROM THE CIRCLE

Last night, when Jalaja invited us to speak, she left space for silence. By then, I think many of us were in an altered state. In such states, there can be long stretches of silence that are very pregnant. Sometimes leaders get uncomfortable with those long silences. They think, "Oh, nobody's saying anything, nothing's happening," and they'll chop it off. I love that Jalaja doesn't do that. In those quiet moments last night, I felt the ancestors come in.

ensconced in the comforts of the familiar. Instead of connecting heart to heart and soul to soul, they would connect mind to mind. So instead, I ask them to maintain complete silence. No chitchat, no small talk.

We Westerners tend to avoid the experience of shared silence, as if needing to fend of the shadows of separation with an incessant stream of words. Yaya Diallo, an African healer who immigrated to Canada, describes his dismay at finding himself among people who never stop talking:

> The Minianka affirm the value of being silent and do not feel an obligation to say everything or to make conversation needlessly. It is disconcerting to be in the company of Westerners who do not know how to appreciate being quietly in someone else's presence. It was a shock to me when I first came to Canada to find that whenever I simply wished to rest quietly within myself, I was hounded with questions. . . . A person who talks too much in Minianka society is not taken seriously and may not even be listened to after a while.[1]

Most tribal peoples understand that too much talking doesn't serve us, nor does it promote fulfilling relationships. When we overdose on words, we become heady and ungrounded. To have true contact with another soul, we have to venture beyond the picket fences we build with our words. As Gandhi put it: "In the attitude of silence the soul finds the path in a clearer light, and what is elusive and deceptive resolves itself into crystal clearness."

Speaking into the quiet space we have created in our circle, I now invite the women to do what I call the *Heart Greeting*. In many of my circles, it's one of the first practices we do. It goes like this:

◎ Face your partner and place your right hand over your part-

VOICES FROM THE CIRCLE

When the flyer for the week-long training came in the mail, it sat on my living room table like a hot potato. I knew I needed to go, but it totally freaked me out. So I told myself I would just go check out this Circlework thing and have a nice time. But it was . . . (*She starts to cry.*) It was so amazing. I cried all through that week because I sensed the ancientness of the energy. It felt so big. I knew I couldn't turn my back on this even though I was scared. I had been so disconnected from my soul and so fearful—fearful of everything, but especially of intimacy. The depth of intimacy I experience here still terrifies me. And yet I yearn for it so much.

ner's heart.

◎ She will do the same.

◎ Then, place your left hand over your *own* heart, covering your partner's hand.

◎ Keep your focus on yourself and on your own experience. Focus less on looking than on feeling. Don't get lost in your partner's eyes. Instead, after a brief moment of eye contact, close your eyes, turn to your heart, and try to sense the connection between your hearts.

◎ Send a blessing for this woman and for your relationship, and allow yourself to receive her blessing. Breathe, and let your hearts be nourished.

◎ Stay together as long as it feels right. Then, very slowly, draw back your hands. Stay in silence as you separate.

◎ Then, begin to walk through the room until you find a new partner.

Once everyone understands the process, we all do it. I too participate and am moved by the unique beauty of each woman's energy. Aside from the fact that nurturing our heart connection in this way feels great, it's also a tonic that is making our circle stronger and more resilient. If, at a later point, conflict should arise, it will be held in the web of love that practices like the Heart Greeting help us create. By opening our hearts in this way, we are laying the foundation for what lies ahead.

After each women has shared the Heart Greeting with three or four others, I invite them to bring their attention back to themselves.

"Complete the greeting you're presently involved with," I say. "Take all the time you need. Then, close your eyes."

"Now, place your hands on your own heart and greet yourself

with the same respect and reverence you offered the other women. Acknowledge what it took for you to get here. Honor your courage and your wisdom. Open to the miracle of our being together, right here, right now, in this beautiful place.

I fall silent, entranced by the rich, velvety presence in the room. Barely twenty minutes have passed since we started. But already, we have crossed over into another world. Our journey together has begun. We have entered into sacred space.

"Welcome," I say softly into the deepening silence.

"Welcome to the circle."

Spaciousness

One day a student asked the great Zen painter Ike no Taiga, "What is the most difficult part of painting?" Taiga said, "The part of the paper where nothing is painted is the most difficult."

Zen parable

Circlework is a spacious practice. We leave space between our words, between activities, between the impulse to speak and the act of speaking. We do this, because we recognize spaciousness as an important key to happiness and fulfilment. To our soul, it's as necessary as oxygen to the body.

In contrast, our ego is terrified of spaciousness, which it equates with emptiness, lack, failure, and death. Our ego hates the fact that space can't be controlled, possessed, or manipulated. And since ours is an ego-dominated culture, it's determined to fight back against the menace of space in the only way it can: By trying to fill it. We cover the land with shopping malls and freeways, clutter and sprawl. We fill our schedules with obligations, our bodies with food and our minds with trivial worries. We believe that having lots of stuff and responsibilities is a sign of success, that bigger is better, and that no matter how much we have, we're always

VOICES FROM THE CIRCLE

When I saw your faces, I felt like I was waking up from a nightmare or coming home from a long exile.

going to need more: more possessions, more activities, fun, sex, spiritual teachings.

We all know what happens when we are consistently deprived of spaciousness. At first, there might be just a slight sense of irritation. Eventually, we start feeling stressed or depressed, and ultimately, we're liable to turn violent. This is why, when you look at a world map, you'll see that the most densely populated regions on the planet, such as Gaza and the West Bank, tend to be besieged by violence.

But though we might associate violent explosions with war zones, they are equally common on our mainstream media. Just switch through the channels on your television, and you'll surely see something getting blown up—a person, a car, or a building.

"Well," you might say, "it's just another sign of our addiction to violence." Perhaps. But might our love of explosions also be a symptom of our desperate need for spaciousness? Of course, blowing things up will never give us the experience we're longing for. Still, a good explosion mimics liberation, breaking out, busting free. It simulates the release of all that pent-up inner pressure, an end to confinement and constriction.

I used to think that the hunger for spaciousness I witnessed in myself and in so many of my sisters was just a Western phenomenon. I assumed, for example, that Arab women didn't struggle with the same pressures. In my fantasy, I saw them sitting together drinking endless cups of sweet mint tea.

How wrong I was! Today, I know they're just as stressed out as we are, if not more so. And having worked with women from India, Kenya, Australia, Brazil and many other countries, I understand that what we're dealing with is a global phenomenon linked to industrialization. Throughout the industrialized world, women will tell you the exact same thing: "I'm too busy. Way, way too busy."

Of course, "too busy" doesn't look the same for everyone. Some

Voices from the Circle

The quiet of this place is so special. Being here, surrounded by nature's beauty, helps me to see how I separate myself from pure being and how much I tend to live in my mind. There is something so magical about the hills and the trees and the birds and the water and the light.

people like to do a lot, others don't. But regardless of whether we have just one or a hundred commitments, if we feel like we can't do the things that make us happy without neglecting other important responsibilities, then we're too busy.

I believe this sense of time scarcity is one of the greatest sources of suffering in our lives today. Despite our supposedly time-saving modern conveniences, we have less time than any previous generation to laugh and play, make music and hang out with friends, wander through a forest or sit by a lake.

Any intelligent fool can make things bigger, more complex, and more violent. It takes a touch of genius—and a lot of courage—to move in the opposite direction.

Albert Einstein[2]

Voices from the Circle

I have been in a space of deep silence since our circle ended. I feel it working within me. There is more space inside, and I am breathing more deeply. I am trying to do less, talk less, make fewer commitments in the midst of my noisy, hectic life.

Overfull schedules translate into overfull brains. And so, we feel rushed, harried, cornered, tense, and contracted. Stress brings out the worst in us, making us bitchy, critical, intolerant, and aggressive. How appropriate that the Chinese character for "busyness" should literally translate as "killing the heart"! Amongst all that mental clutter, our heart has no room to breathe. Instead of making us happier, our materialistic way of life is causing an epidemic of stress-related physical and mental ailments.

In Circlework, we honor our need for spaciousness. Allowing stillness and space to blossom in the circle enables us to hear the voice of the heart more clearly, enjoy our beauty more fully, and feel our love more deeply. A subtle surge of pleasure arises and a gentle, luminous ecstasy washes through us. Finally, we can let go of busyness, relax and just listen to the sweet hum of silence.

A beautiful bowl doesn't need to be filled with objects. The same is true of a circle: it, too, does not need to be filled with words. If we want, we can just sit together quietly, in silence. But should thoughts, emotions or stories rise up, asking to be shared, we can voice them, offering them into the bowl of our circle like delicious fruits. Even as a bowl accepts and holds whatever we place into it, so the circle holds and accepts our offerings. In doing so, it reminds us that we, too, are capable of holding and accepting whatever life brings us, even when it's messy, painful or terrifying.

At times, we're bound to lose touch with that inner spaciousness, bound to get lost in the stories and emotions, bound to forget all about the bowl that's holding them all. But sooner or later, we wake up. Then, our attention returns to the beautiful, simple shape of the circle, and to its quiet, open presence. In those moments, it's easy to see why the Sufi mystic Rumi compares our soul to a bowl:

> At dawn I walked along with a monk
> on his way to the monastery.
> We do the same work, I told him.
> We suffer the same.
> He gave me a bowl, and I saw:
> The soul has *this* shape.[3]

This shape, this soul-bowl, this mandala, is what, in Circlework, we are seeking to embody. Of course, we are always embodying space— our bodies are, after all, fields of space. But most of the time, we ignore this fact, like fish who ignore the water they swim through. But there comes a moment when we awaken to the presence of space, both within and around us. As our attention shifts from our dramas to the space within which they arise, we realize that we are, in fact, space awakening to itself.

Eckhart Tolle, one of the great spiritual teachers of our times, describes us as addicted to what he calls "object-consciousness." Externally, we're obsessed with "things," internally with ideas, beliefs and thoughts. But the moment we become aware of the inner space in which they arise, we awaken from the delusional trance of object-consciousness and begin to live in what Tolle calls "space-consciousness".

The circle is the ideal tool for helping us make this shift from object to space-consciousness. Mathematically, a circle is simply the most efficient way of enclosing space. Space is, in other words, its very essence. Every time we reconnect with the circle, it whispers, "Look, this is what you too are. Space is your essential nature. You too are a mandala, a shimmering field of conscious presence, mystery and magic."

At this time in history, evolution is demanding, in no uncertain terms, that we awaken from the trance of object-consciousness. Clearly, nature can no longer sustain our addiction to "stuff." However, this shift also satisfies the deepest yearning of our own hearts and souls. Trapped in a busy, overcrowded world, we dream of spaciousness as captive hawks might dream of soaring through the clean blue air. We yearn for endless beaches and deep forests, quiet mountain lakes and vast prairies, for unscheduled days and weeks, months and years.

In Circlework, we take such desires seriously. We don't dismiss them as temporary moods or passing whims. Mindful of what our hearts and souls are asking for, we commit to cultivating spaciousness—in our own consciousness, in our circles, and in our lives.

As I just mentioned, a circle is mathematically the simplest way of enclosing space. You'd think, then, that all circle gatherings would be interested in exploring states of inner and outer spaciousness. Actually, very few are. Most focus exclusively on what is happening in the circle, and on the stories, emotions and thoughts that are being shared.

There's nothing wrong with this, it just isn't Circlework. In fact, the spaciousness of the process is a major key to its transformational power—a fact that by the end of our week together, every woman in our training circle will understand. As one participant puts it:

What makes Circlework so powerful isn't what fills the circle space. That has become very clear to me. It's the emptiness, the

VOICES FROM THE CIRCLE

The first time I came to a circle, I thought, wow, I've never done anything besides marijuana that felt like this. Everything feels so intense. That was years ago. Now, I've been doing Circlework for so long that I live that way throughout my days. I feel so comfortable in myself. I no longer fret and worry whether others will approve of me.

removal of so much that is not necessary and not needed. It's the silence, and the open spaciousness. We have a lot of silence, not only in declared times, but silence and quiet that is allowed between things, between exercises or between people's words. In the empty space, presence arises. I have learned to trust in that silence, and in the fullness that results from it. I have learned that less is more.

Not only is the circle process spacious and slow, but there's lots of "down" time between circle meetings for women to nap, go for walks or tend to their inner process. Often, it is during these quiet times that the most important seeds of change are sown. These hours of dreaming, journaling and meditating, of solitude and silence, allow us to dive deep within and connect with our true needs and desires.

As we absorb the healing medicine of spaciousness, peace returns to our hearts and minds, until finally, there is nothing more to say, nothing left to do. At last, we can rest. Instead of trying so hard to prove our worth, we allow ourselves to be who we are. Our natural gentleness emerges as we hang out by the well, drinking the waters of life.

The Courage to Stop

My work has convinced me that the solidarity and sisterhood of women worldwide is an essential key to healing our communities. Most women understand that violence and war are not the answer. They know the power of vulnerability and the importance of good communication. They recognize the rational mind as a useful but limited tool and are willing to listen to their intuition. They are also, in my experience, immensely courageous. When women join forces to protect Mother Earth and her children, they become an unstoppable force.

However, to be truly effective, we must overcome certain addictions that our society has foisted upon us—first and foremost, the addiction to incessant thinking and doing.

In my circles, I regularly meet amazing women who are doing incredible work in the world. Yet many say they're feeling tired, burned out, exhausted. Some, like those I work with in the Middle East, live in war zones. Most do not. But outer peace does not guarantee inner peace. We all know what it feels like to be shackled to the incessantly turning wheels of our mind. We know how easily our incessant thoughts, worries, and emotions can create a tangled web that obscures the ever-present ground of peace. We know what it's like to get caught up in a million projects and goals that contribute little to our happiness.

We can't help that now and then, we lose ourselves amidst the craziness of modern life. But when that happens, can we honestly acknowledge it? When we feel stressed, overwhelmed, or assaulted by despair, can we face what we're feeling and give ourselves permission to slow down, stop, and retreat?

Unfortunately, our society classifies taking time to slow down and re-center as a luxury, rather than a necessity. Therefore women often feel guilty for taking the space and time they need. They believe they should always be active, productive, useful and of service.

Yet the truth is that when we're feeling stressed and overwhelmed, we rarely do much good and may even unwittingly cause harm. To see clearly where our path lies, we must step back, sit quietly and take time to ask the important questions that so often get shoved aside in daily life: Why am I here? What is my purpose in life? What are my highest values? Am I living in alignment with them? Is my heart happy? Is my soul content?

For any woman who wants to lead a passionate, fulfilling life, taking time to explore such questions is no luxury but a basic necessity. Circlework provides a place where she can do this. In the circle, she can come home to herself, rest, re-center, find her innate balance and restore her depleted energies. Here, spaciousness is not incidental.

Rather, it's structured into the process. There are periods of silence. There's time for rest and introspection. The process flows in an easy, unpressured way. After a good circle, even our faces look different: softer, younger, and more open.

Circlework is a Practice

When women first experience the magic of Circlework, they wonder whether perhaps, it was just a fluke, a lucky coincidence. But then they return and find that once again, their loneliness recedes and is replaced by hope, inspiration and connection. Eventually, they come to understand that, yes, the magic can indeed be replicated. There are tools, guidelines, and practices. Use them with the right intentions, and the magic happens.

Usually, people first experience Circlework in the context of a workshop or retreat. But Circlework is not really meant to be a once-in-a-lifetime experience. Rather, the key to embodying the mandala in our daily lives is repetition. Of course, this is true of any spiritual practice. Devout Catholics don't just go to church once, and then never again. They go over and over, until the seeds of their faith grow deep roots.

We might leave a Circlework retreat filled with light and peace. But over time, it's easy to dragged back into the muck. Here, a young woman called Alina talks about this:

Last year I stumbled into the circle. I was completely terrified all through it. At one point, I wanted to leave, and almost did. But I made it through, and I felt completely changed. Then I went back to my world, and tried to keep what I had learned in the circle alive, and give it to other people. But I wasn't strong enough to do it alone. Throughout this year, I have watched myself die slowly. *(She weeps)*. I want to keep this way of being with me always. After the last circle there was a deep loneliness. How do I keep this feeling with me?

Another woman called Kim responds by saying:

Alina, I so hear you. I've been doing Circlework for several years now, and in my experience, it takes more than one circle. Integrating these teachings is a process. Even though people change in just one circle, you don't really understand the radically transformative nature of this work right away. I personally needed to immerse myself in the practice, and I needed to be in the circle long enough to really make it part of who I am.

Marina agrees with Kim and adds:

Now, I'm living Circlework. It's everywhere in my life. There's a continuity of my connection with Spirit, and with the sacred. I hold sacred space wherever I go. I have learned how to be more connected with other people, so I'm no longer so isolated. I feel much stronger and more powerful, but in a gentle way. I'm more aware of my strength and less judgmental of my weaknesses.

The first time we consciously experience the healing medicine of Circlework, it's like planting a seed. Then, we keep nurturing and watering that seed until it begins to sprout and grow deep roots within our being. Eventually, the circle becomes part of our very being, an inner friend whom we can call on at any time. The mere remembrance of the circle instantly calls forth the knowledge of our wholeness. The journey to the center has become a path we've taken so many times that we know it well. Even at night, in the dark, we can find it.

Seven Steps to Recreating the Magic

Right now, you might feel light years removed from the serene, peaceful retreat center where the Circlework Training was held. And yet, I want to assure you that wherever you are, you too can access the sense of spaciousness and sacredness we enjoyed in our circle. To recreate the magic, you need only follow the same six steps that we took in our circles. Let's take a look at what they were.

1 We scheduled time out.

To nurture your soul, you *must* be willing to take some time out of your busy life. Maybe you can't take a week right now. But can you take five minutes? Of course you can. Everyone has five minutes. So would you be willing to start setting aside five minutes every morning? Five minutes to simply sit quietly and be present? To bless yourself and honor your soul? Five minutes to feel yourself cradled in love and bathed in light? Give it a try. It's amazing what a difference five minutes a day can make!

2 We stopped.

All day long, we think, talk, and do. To enter sacred space, we need to be willing to let all that go and come to a full stop. That is precisely what we did in our circle. We switched from thinking to listening, from talking to silence and from doing to being.

You too can do this. When you take your five minutes, don't spend them thinking, planning, worrying and reminiscing. Make a strong commitment to stop and just be, like a beautiful tree standing in the meadow, nourished by the earth and bathed in light.

3 We connected with the circle.

The circle is what the great psychologist CG Jung called an *archetype*. What this means is that it's not just an external geometric form but also an inner source of healing, wisdom and power. Gathering in a circle is one way to connect with that inner resource. However, there are many others, such as painting mandalas or simply visualizing them. This book will help you forge that connection, so that you can invoke the healing power of the circle whenever you want. For now, just affirm your willingness to open to the circle as a friend and ally.

4 We opened to nature.

Whenever possible, I try to hold my circles in places where we can easily tune into nature. We can't always be in places of great natural beauty. Still, no matter where we are, there is always a way to connect with nature. To the soul, communion with nature is not a luxury but a necessity. So don't begrudge it what it needs. Take that walk. Sit with that tree. Go visit that beach. Hang out with your cat. Stop, for just a moment, to listen to the wind and the rain.

5 We engaged the body.

Whenever we want to step out of mental busyness into peaceful stillness, the body is our best ally. In our circle, we listened to beautiful music. We danced and touched. Your situation may be very different, but no matter where you are, you too can find a way to tap the wisdom of your body. Do that Yoga routine. Turn on your music and dance. Take a moment to lovingly caress your own face. Say hi to the goddess within. Speak kindly to yourself, and welcome yourself into sacred space.

6 We opened our hearts with clear intention.

This step is important. In fact, it may well be most important one of all. Typically, we open our hearts only when certain conditions are met. In Circlework, on the other hand, we hold a conscious intention of doing so *all the time.*

This is something you too can do. Place your hands on your chest and try to feel your heart. Breathe into it. Invite it to relax, to soften and open. Remind yourself that you are safe. Affirm that you are in the presence of love. Though your mind may argue, some part of you knows this to be true. Remind yourself, over and over, that love is here, will always be here, and has been knocking on your door since the beginning of time.

These seven steps are ones that you too can take. Do so, and you too will be cradled in sacred space. Feel yourself now, resting in the bowl of the circle, the bowl of this moment which is sacred, infinite and magical.

CHAPTER 2

CREATING FIELDS OF LOVE

*A circle of trust is a group of people who know how to sit quietly
. . . with each other and wait for the shy soul to show up. The
relationships in such a group are not pushy but patient; they are
not confrontational but compassionate; they are filled not with
expectations and demands but with abiding faith in the reality of
the inner teacher and in each person's capacity to learn from it.*

Parker Palmer[1]

VOICES FROM THE CIRCLE

That feeling of safety,
of deep permission to
be exactly who I am is
so special. Often, I look
around at us dancing, or
at someone speaking or
listening. I look, and I
think, "This is what love
looks like. Yes, this is what
love looks like."

This love—I don't know
if it breaks my heart or if
it is breaking me open; I
can't tell.

When it comes to magic, nobody rivals Mother Nature. Crocuses pushing up through the snow, sunsets and moon rises, orgasms and babies—there's no end to it.

But we too are part of nature, and we too are magicians. We make magic every time we open our hearts to love or allow ourselves to be used as instruments of healing. This kind of magic—magic sourced in the realm of the sacred—is what Circlework is all about. In this chapter, I want to tell you a story about a woman who was healed by the magic of the circle. Betty was a short, stocky, woman in her fifties. Ten years ago, her husband's death had plunged her into a deep depression from which she had yet to emerge. Psychologists and psychiatrists had tried their best to crack the hard shell of her withdrawal—all in vain. Her eyes were dull, her shoulders drooped and her whole body seemed to say, "I don't want to be here."

I met Betty at the beginning of a five-day retreat that she had signed up for. But why, I wondered? She didn't seem to want to be here. She didn't seem to want to be *anywhere*. When I asked her why she decided to come, she shrugged despondently. "I'm not sure . . . Honestly, I don't know."

Ten years is an awfully long time to be seriously depressed, and I doubted the circle would make a dent in Betty's condition. Sometimes, people come to the circle with wounds so deep they can't be touched. Betty was surely one of them. She was too far gone, too deeply immersed in her own world, too accustomed to being sad and hopeless. On breaks, she made no attempt to talk to anyone, and though she was civil to those who approached her, she seemed absent, as if her soul had flown the coop, leaving behind a mere husk.

But Circlework creates a powerful vortex of love. In fact, one of my favorite definitions is this: *Circlework is the art of gathering in circles to create fields of love powerful enough to heal us, our communities, and our world.*

The field of love that we create astonishes me. As a gardener I know about trees, I know about the field of energy trees create. But to be in a field of human love has been huge for me. The energy we generate when we open our hearts is incredible.

Of course, we're not talking about romantic love here. This isn't the spot-beam kind of love that singles out one person while ignoring everyone else. It's more like the warm sunlight that blesses everything it touches. And as we soon learned, even Betty was not immune to that warmth.

By coincidence, I found out that Betty's birthday was going to fall on the fifth day of our circle. The group included a group of teenage girls, and when they heard of Betty's upcoming birthday, they told me they wanted to do something special for her.

"Fine," I said.

VOICES FROM THE CIRCLE

Once my therapist told me, "Well, you have to love yourself." I said, "I *do* love myself, but there seems to be a limit, a cap, and to go beyond it I need to see love reflected in a genuine way in other people. I need to have an experience of being totally loved in order to get to the next level." Circlework has given me that. Because the love is so intimate, yet there are no sexual implications and no demands.

What I received from Circlework was a beam of love so powerful that I was just floored. I never dreamed such love was possible. And it has absolutely nothing to do with the kind of love that's celebrated in songs and movies. It's something else entirely.

On the morning of Betty's birthday, we all gathered in the wood-beamed lodge. As usual, I opened with music, poetry and movement. Then, I turned matters over to the four young girls. I had no idea what they had planned and was as curious as everyone else. All I knew was that early that morning, I'd seen them gathering flowers in a nearby meadow.

Voices from the Circle

I'm happily married, with four children and seven grandkids, and I feel surrounded by divine presence. How could I possibly want more? But for most of my life, I did, because I longed to experience human love in a fuller way. Well, this week, in this circle, I received the human love I've been hungering for for so long. I am so deeply grateful. I've been heard and seen and birthed in a whole new way.

First, Annie, a slender girl with long, silky brown hair, turned to Betty. "Betty," she said, "I'd like you to step into the circle."

Startled yet willing, Betty stood up and complied.

"Now," said Rhiannon, a gentle, soft-spoken young girl, "we need you to close your eyes."

Betty did.

"No peeking!" Rhiannon added sternly. "You can't open your eyes till we say so."

Then, amidst giggles and a flurry of excitement, the girls produced a cake, complete with candles and icing. How they had managed that was a mystery to me, for our center was in the middle of nowhere. In addition to the cake, they also had a bag, and out of it, they pulled a stunning garland woven of yellow, purple and red blossoms.

Once all the candles were lit, the girls told Betty to open her eyes. As she did, one girl walked up with the blazing cake, while a second gently placed the flower garland around her neck.

"Oh my God, they're fairies," I found myself thinking. And indeed, they looked like sweet young fairies come to bless their grandmother.

Of course, they were simply young girls expressing their caring in the best way they knew how. At the same time, what they did was quintessentially feminine. Everything traditionally associated with the goddess Aphrodite was right there: laughter and play, flowers, sweetness, beauty and pleasure.

I will never forget what happened next. First, there was complete silence. I expected Betty to say, "How nice, thank you," or something of that sort.

Instead, she said not a word. Standing still as a rock, her face started shifting and transforming before her eyes. Under her skin, sheets of ice seemed to be melting and cracking, as if after months of wintry darkness the sun had risen and was caressing her with warm fingers. Her eyes lit up and joy shone from her cheeks.

Still, she didn't speak, *couldn't* speak. Instead, overcome with emotion, she started gasping. For at least five minutes straight, Betty just gasped with ecstatic joy like a child far too excited to speak. The entire circle sat in rapt attention. Many of us felt goose bumps of wonder as we watched her.

From that moment on, Betty was radiant. Every trace of depression was gone. I could hardly believe that such a complete turnaround was possible, let alone that it had been accomplished by something as simple as a birthday cake and a flower garland.

But of course, the cake and the garland weren't really the magic ingredients. Like all real magic, what happened that day was powered by love.

Love is powerful. Kindness heals. We all know this, and most of us do our best to be kind, especially if we're on a spiritual path. Still, we have our doubts. What about all the people who aren't loving or kind? Most of them seem to do just fine. How much of a difference can our small acts of love really make?

I can assure you, without a doubt, that they make an enormous difference. In daily life, it's often hard to tell. But a circle is like a little petri dish. The experiments we conduct there have taught me, beyond a shadow of a doubt, that love really is the most potent healing force at our disposal.

Of course, love is a much abused and overused word. Still, when all is said and done, it's what Circlework is all about. Love is the force that sustains the circles of our lives and mends them when they shatter. It's what transforms our circles into bowls that can hold whatever we put into it: the light and the dark, the joyful laughter and the heart-rending wails of despair. Love, in this

Voices from the Circle

In the circle we get to know each other in a very intimate way. We might not know what someone's job is or where they live, but we get to see their real essence. I'm still dumbfounded at how magnificent this process is.

Every time I come to a week-long circle, I reach a point when I experience being completely accepted and loved. The truth is, prior to Circlework, I never had that experience. I was into my fifties before I had the experience of being loved in that unconditional way. Every time it happens I feel like it would be okay to die. I don't want to die, but I feel it would be okay now. It's such a wonderful feeling. Death has become less fearful now that I've been loved so fully.

sense, is not just a fuzzy feeling, but a spiritual practice, an art, a skill, and a discipline. There's much to learn, and everything we learn needs to be practiced over and over, until it becomes integrated into the very marrow of our being.

Love rarely enters us all at once, sweeping away our old wounds and contractions like a great tidal wave. More often, it trickles in slowly but surely, over time, until the inner dam bursts and the life-giving water comes flooding in. By the time Betty's birthday arrived, she'd been resting in the oasis of our circle for days. She'd been bathed in the waters of love. She'd been held and rocked, sung to and cherished. Slowly, the grip of her depression had loosened. On the day of her birthday blessing, that final nudge was all it took for her depression to relinquish its hold.

To witness this happening was an experience I shall never forget. We all felt like we were present to a miracle—and so we were, for the healing power of a love-infused circle is nothing less than miraculous. Yet as memorable as Betty's birthday celebration was, such outpourings of kindness are by no means unusual. I have led thousands of circles and have yet to experience one where women did not demonstrate the most extraordinary capacity for love. They aren't just "being nice," which can imply a falseness, a discrepancy between what we say and what we really feel. Rather, they're demonstrating the sincere caring that wells up from the heart like cool, clear water.

Once you've witnessed such events, not just once but repeatedly, you can no longer be fooled. You know then, that kindness and love aren't just the icing on the cake of life. Without them, there would be no cake at all. Love is what knits the circumference of our circle together and allows us to embrace each other despite our infuriating quirks, our weirdness and our brokenness. Just as water can transform the desert into a carpet of flowers, so love can transform even the most barren inner landscape into a green, verdant oasis.

VOICES FROM THE CIRCLE

My question for the last few days has been, how much more can I hold of all this love and sweetness? At one point, I wanted to check out, but I stayed. I held it. I've grown big enough to hold it. I want to open and open and open to this love, it feels so wonderful and juicy, like honey to a bee. I just want to roll in that honey and take it home with me and spread it all over everything.

It all comes down to love, doesn't it? We all want the same thing. Watching these women connect with themselves, and finding the connection between their heart and their body and their soul . . . It just . . . There are no words. It just fills me with compassion.

Kindness Practice

The girls who planned Betty's birthday ritual used food, candles, flowers. They braided kindness with beauty, and beauty with respect.

In this practice, you're going to do something similar for yourself. Your first step is to schedule at least a full hour during the next week that will be dedicated to celebrating yourself in a way that is not only kind but also sensual and delicious.

Once you've scheduled your time, your next task is to decide what you are going to do. Here are a few examples of how women have chosen to celebrate themselves:

◎ I drew myself a wonderful bath with lavender salts and rose petals. I lit many candles and took a leisurely bath, and all the while I spoke kind words to myself.

◎ I made myself a cup of tea. Then I sat in the window seat and just watched the birds outside. For once, I didn't berate myself for doing nothing. Instead, I just kept reminding myself to enjoy, enjoy, enjoy.

◎ I went and got my nails done. The whole time, I kept sweet-talking myself: "Honey, I love you. You're beautiful, sweetie-pie."

◎ I took a slow walk in the woods and talked to the trees.

CHAPTER 3

WORKING WITH MANDALA POWER

There is geometry in the humming of the strings, there is music in the spacing of the spheres.

Pythagoras

Spider webs and birds' nests, suns and moons—nature's love of circles is obvious. No wonder, then, that circles also feature large in works of prehistoric art around the world, some of which date back no less than 300 000 years. In the eyes of most indigenous peoples, the circle was a sacred and immensely powerful form. Just think, for example, of the huge stone circles erected by the ancient Celts across Europe, or of the healing circles used by shamans on every continent. Around the world, our ancestors treasured the circle as a potent tool for healing and awakening and developed a wide range of unique ways to tap the powers of the circle.

Asked about the values of his culture, the circle was the first thing that the great Sioux chief Black Elk talked about. "You have noticed that everything an Indian does is done in a circle," he said:

And that is because the Power of the World always works in circles, and everything tries to be round. This knowledge came to us from the outer world with our religion. Everything the Power of the World does is done in a circle. The sky is round, and I have heard that the earth is round like a ball, and so are all the stars.

The wind, in its greatest power, whirls. Birds make their nests in circles, for theirs is the same religion as ours. The sun comes forth and goes down again in a circle. The moon does the same, and both are round. Even the seasons form a great circle in their changing, and always come back again to where they were. The life of a man is a circle from childhood to childhood, and so it is in everything where power moves. Our teepees were round like the nests of birds, and these were always set in a circle, the nation's hoop, a nest of many nests, where the Great Spirit meant for us to hatch our children.[1]

In the West, too, the circle has always been associated with divine perfection. When, for example, the 17th century artist and poet William Blake wanted to capture the miracle of creation, he painted the gray-bearded patriarch leaning down from heaven, compass in hand, poised to draw the great arc of the cosmos. God's compass is, in Blake's rendering, a rather primitive contraption, much like what children around the world use even today. Yet as he knew well, a compass is, despite its simplicity, a magical little tool and an instrument worthy of God's touch. One leg remains still, the other moves, and out of this dance of movement and stillness, creation is born.

In Circlework, two ancient and universal lineages unite. On the one hand, we're following in the footsteps of the countless peoples who, through the ages, used circle gatherings to strengthen and unite their communities.

On the other, we also stand in the lineage of all the visionaries, mystics, healers, and artists who revered the circle as a timeless expression of divine perfection and used it as a tool for awakening and healing. We too approach the circle as a mandala—which is to say, a doorway into sacred space and a blueprint of our own essential wholeness.

As a format for group gatherings, the circle can help us restore our fractured communities. But viewed as a mandala, it reflects our own

VOICES FROM THE CIRCLE

For me as an African American, one of the great gifts of the circle is that it has awakened a sense of connection with my African ancestors. I started dreaming of African queens and priestesses and feeling their groundedness in the earth and the elements. It feels like a memory, not like something I read in books. It comes from a whole other dimension.

intrinsic wholeness and serves as a source of physical, emotional and spiritual healing. This dual use of the circle as a medicine that heals not only our relationships and communities but also our souls is an important aspect of what makes Circlework such a powerful transformational tool.

What is a Mandala?

In Circlework, we approach the circle as a mandala. But what exactly does that word mean? Based on the stacks of mandala coloring books that adorn every bookstore, you might be forgiven for assuming that a mandala is just a circle that's been subdivided in some more or less meaningful sort of way. In fact, nothing could be further from the truth.

Mandala is a Sanskrit word generally translated as "sacred circle." Though originally used in the context of Hindu and Buddhist philosophy, it's now widely applied to any circle used in healing or spiritual practice.

Though a mandala is a circle, it can also integrate other shapes. The circle is, after all, not the only geometric form to which special powers have been attributed. In many traditions, it's believed that *all* geometric forms have inherent meaning and power, and that together, they form a kind of sacred language. This belief underlies the field of study known as *sacred geometry*. Sacred geometry plays an important role in many world religions, such as Hinduism and Buddhism, where certain shapes and colors correspond to specific deities.

Mandalas can range from very simple to extremely complex. Some of the most intricate ones can be found in Islamic art, works of breathtaking splendor birthed by a religious tradition that has long cherished geometry as a sacred language. At the other end of the spectrum we have mandalas painted by Zen masters with a single brushstroke. Clear expressions of enlightened consciousness, they remind us that just as great poets can convey profound messages using

VOICES FROM THE CIRCLE

At first, I couldn't relate to the sacred geometry stuff. It seemed so abstract. Now, it's in my body. I feel it all the time, not just when I'm in circle. Where's my center? Am I in my heaven-earth axis? Once I remember the mandala I can relax and get grounded. The knowledge is no longer just mental, I'm embodying it.

only the simplest words, so the potency of a mandala does not depend on its complexity.

Today, we no longer think of geometry as a sacred art. Yet through the ages, it was seen as a window into the mind of God, capable of revealing the blueprint behind everything from nests and flowers to solar systems and galaxies. On the one hand, sacred geometry tries to decode the hidden messages within the forms we see. On the other, it explores how we might use these forms to heal our consciousness and to shift our vibrational frequency towards the sacred, the holy and the divine. As Spirit blesses and touches us through certain geometric forms, so we in turn can use them to attune our consciousness to that of the Creator.

Many traditions have developed a sophisticated understanding of the symbolism of various geometric forms such as squares and triangles, octagons and octahedrons. Within a true mandala, these elements are never purely ornamental. Rather, they are like the verbs and nouns that make up the language of sacred geometry. Decipher that language, and you have a set of teachings as profound and encompassing as any religious scripture. Indeed, in many traditions, certain mandalas are viewed as sacred scriptures, written in the language of form.

One example is the Kalachakra mandala, which plays a central role in Tibetan Buddhism. Kalachakra (literally, "wheel of time") is the name of the central deity who presides over the mandala. However, it also refers to the state of omniscient consciousness that the mandala is designed to awaken within us.

I'm fortunate to live in a town where a group of Tibetan monks periodically construct the Kalachakra mandala. Its creation and destruction is a ritual reserved for monks who have undergone years of training. Enormous skill is called for, not only because of the immense complexity of the design, which portraits no less than 722 deities, but also because the mandala consists of tiny grains of colored sand dispensed from open-ended cones.

The process of creating the mandala takes weeks, and is usually performed in a public place where the community can watch. And watch they do. They seem to sense that what they're receiving is a form of spiritual medicine that links them directly to the realm of the sacred and has a powerfully beneficial impact on their body, mind and spirit.

Teenage kids and old men, mothers and children—all stand silently, mesmerized by the sight of the red-robed monks laboring with total concentration as the great mandala takes shape. In this process, the artistic value of the mandala is secondary. What matters, above all, is the monks' state of inner alignment and centeredness. Long before they begin working on the mandala, they meditate, pray and chant.

To gaze at the Kalachakra mandala is to contemplate a map that portrays the cosmos and the powers that govern it, organized as an integrated whole around a spiritual center. It's a map of creation, but also of our inner landscape. It shows us where the path to wholeness lies, while at the same time reminding us that wholeness is already our essential nature.

When one feels lost, as so many people do today, the appearance of such a map can be profoundly calming and reassuring. No matter how chaotic our situation might be, the great mandala assures us that there really is a divine order, and that we are part of it. Just as an anxious child calms down in the arms of a loving mother, the mandala helps our fearful psyche to relax.

But then, after weeks or even months of labor, the monks ritually destroy their creation: The true mandala is not the visible one. Rather, it's a vortex of sacred energy that continues to bless the world long after its physical form has vanished.

Indeed, no physical mandala we create, be it sculpted, painted or embodied, is ever the true mandala. In the physical world, we have only two or, at best, three dimensions to work with. Yet what our mandala actually represents is a multi-dimensional reality within which everything is interconnected in ways that far transcend the scope of our intellect. The physical mandala is merely a pointer towards something that originates in the realm of light and consciousness. This is why, when used as spiritual medicine, mandalas can lead us beyond mind and ego into the vastness of our true nature.

Going as a River

It's one thing to use a mandala as a map or as a sacred scripture. But the moment we chose to *embody* it, as we do in Circlework, we face a new challenge. For as long as we experience ourselves as a group of separate individuals, our mandala will have no circumference. We're like a bunch of dots, hinting at the possibility of a true circumference, yet without actually manifesting it. To actually constellate the circumference, we'll have to unite. Of course, our bodies will remain separate, but on the level of consciousness, our sense of separation needs to dissolve.

The Vietnamese activist Thich Nhat Hanh says it beautifully:

Despair is a great temptation in our century. Alone, we are vulnerable. If we try to go to the ocean as a single drop of water, we will evaporate before we even arrive. But if we go as a river, if we go as a community, we are sure to arrive at the ocean.[2]

But what exactly does that mean—to "go as a river"? Thich Nhat Hanh seems to be implying, not just that we need to cooperate, but that on some level, we need to actually merge, like droplets of water united by their desire to reach the ocean.

Well. According to Western science, this isn't possible; we're not capable of merging like water drops. We're separate beings, each with our own body, mind and emotions.

But Thich Nhat Hanh is not only an activist, but also a spiritual teacher, and spirituality has always insisted that we aren't as separate as we've been led to believe. Mystics of all traditions assure us that our consciousness is actually quite capable of fusing, not only with that of another person or group, but also with the whole cosmos.

Even Einstein dismissed our apparent separateness as nothing but an optical illusion.

Most scientists have long poo-pooed the very notion of collective consciousness. The idea of separation was, after all, fundamental to Newtonian physics. But in recent years, this has been changing. Certain species, we've been realizing, really do seem to know how to "go like a river."

Ants, for example. Clearly, an ant colony is governed by a source of intelligence that doesn't reside in any individual ant. "Ants aren't smart, says Deborah M. Gordon, a biologist at Stanford University. "Ant colonies are." In a National Geographic feature, Peter Miller summarizes the riddle that scientists are puzzling over:

> Such as finding the shortest path to the best food source, allocating workers to different tasks, or defending a territory from neighbors. As individuals, ants might be tiny dummies, but as colonies they respond quickly and effectively to their environment.
>
> Where this intelligence comes from raises a fundamental question in nature: How do the simple actions of individuals add up to the complex behavior of a group? How do hundreds of honeybees make a critical decision about their hive if many of them disagree? What enables a school of herring to coordinate its movements so precisely it can change direction in a flash, like a single, silvery organism? The collective abilities of such animals—none of which grasps the big picture, but each of which contributes to the group's success—seem miraculous even to the biologists who know them best.[3]

It's clear that being able to merge their consciousness gives ants, and many other species, a tremendous advantage. After all, a group that can move as one has a far better chance of surviving than a bunch of separate individuals, all pulling in different directions.

But the truly extraordinary thing is not that certain creatures know how to form a united collective. Rather, it's the fact that in doing so, they gain access to *a completely new order of intelligence*—an intelligence which, on their own, none of them possess.

Naturally, this begs the question: Might this be true of us, too? Might we, too, be able to join forces in ways that could give us access to potentially life-saving knowledge and wisdom?

Certainly, our indigenous ancestors believed this was the case. Through rituals that might involve dancing, chanting, drumming and plant medicines, they dissolved their ordinary ego-boundaries and opened to otherwise inaccessible sources of guidance. This, they felt, was important, not just for the health of individuals but for the community as a whole.

Today, in a time of global crisis, it would be foolish not to ask ourselves whether perhaps, we too might have the capacity to tune into sources of guidance and intelligence that individually, we can't access. Might we, by connecting with these sources, be able to serve our suffering planet far more effectively?

Certainly, what I've experienced in my circles would support this view. Whenever I witness a woman receiving a piece of guidance that will change her life, and the lives of many others, I ask myself, where does it come from? Some will say it comes from the soul, or from Spirit. But personally, I believe there is a source of intelligence and wisdom that belongs to us collectively, and that we can only access together, in community.

In our circles, we often experience a coming together and a sense of union that is hard to describe. We don't lose our sense of personal integrity. On the contrary, in those moments of union, we feel completely ourselves, complete whole. We remain who we are, but at the same time, we expand into a bigger, more expansive consciousness. Often, we find that this expanded self is far more intelligent than our ordinary self. It's wiser, more courageous and more inspired.

Going as a river makes sense, then. It's not just that united, we're stronger, but that together, we gain access to a collective

VOICES FROM THE CIRCLE

I was in a really old, painful place. And then, all of a sudden I realized I had the circle there with me even though I was alone, and that knowledge made me extremely happy. I knew it was something I could call upon at any time. I believe that at some level, every circle I have ever connected with is available to me. It is never lost.

consciousness that knows far more and is much wiser than our personal consciousness.

As Lynne McTaggart has clearly demonstrated with her "intention experiment," the power of consciousness is real. When a group of people focus on a common healing intention, the results can be measured and are statistically significant. To spiritual seekers, this comes as no surprise. Yet McTaggart has done us a huge favor by demonstrating, in a way even the most scientifically minded skeptic will find difficult to ignore, that consciousness is a reality we would be foolish to dismiss, and that joining forces is the key to using the power of intention effectively.[4]

To this, I would add that through skillful use of the mandala we can greatly amplify and intensify this power. Whenever we want to "go as a river," the mandala is our best friend and ally. This is, I suspect, why in the circle, our shared prayers are so often answered in astounding ways. Like a megaphone amplifies our voices, so the mandala amplifies our intentions. Of course, indigenous peoples around the world have long known this. In many traditions, the first step to broadcasting their prayers to the universe was always to gather in a circle.

The Circle: A Symbol for Our Times

◎ The circle belongs equally to all peoples. No matter what our cultural heritage is, the circle links us to the traditions of our ancestors.

◎ The circle is an inherently democratic symbol, for it reminds us that like points on the circumference of a circle, we are different yet equal.

◎ Universally, the circle represents unity, connection, and interconnection—all keys to peace in the global era.

◎ The circle affirms what we are capable of becoming: Centered, integrated, and whole.

◎ Because the circle has served as a symbol of wholeness, one-ness, and sacredness for thousands of years, our understanding of it is not just cultural but instinctual.

◎ The circle reflects the shape of the planet and is therefore an apt symbol for a species that recognizes the oneness of planet Earth.

◎ Unlike most religious symbols, the circle was created not by man but by nature. As such, it calls us to approach nature with reverence and respect.

Awakening the Circle Archetype

In Western psychology, C.G. Jung was one of the first to remember and reclaim the long forgotten power of sacred geometry in service of mental healing. Realizing just how ancient and how universal our reverence for circles is, he called the circle the archetype of wholeness, of divinity, and of the Self.

Archetypes, he explained, are images that our species has lived with for so long that they've become embedded in our collective consciousness. To use modern imagery, we might say they're part of the psychological hardware we are born with. Just as a baby instinctively recognizes and responds to the mother, so the circle evokes in us a natural movement towards healing and wholeness. Even people who have never heard of a mandala intuitively understand its message of balance, unity and sanctity. The circle archetype is, in other words, a kind of inner medicine that can help us stay balanced and peaceful, even in the midst of severe threats to our wholeness.

There's just one problem. Archetypes are much like electric power generators, in the sense that they need to be "switched on" in order to serve us. Around the world, this is always done in the same way: By focusing on the geometric elements of the circle. Sacred geometry is the switch that activates the circle archetype within us, which is also why in Circlework, we pay so much attention to it. Regular engagement with the mandala and its geometric elements reconnects us with what, deep down, we all know but often forget: that we are not broken but whole, not separate but connected.

In ancient times, our ancestors used a wide range of circle-based practices to ensure that the circle archetype stayed active and alive in their psyche. We, on the other hand, no longer do. We don't live in round yurts or tipis. We rarely dance in the round, meditate on mandalas, or erect stone circles and labyrinths. And so, the circle archetype lies dormant in our psyche, like a tool that's been rusting in the basement for so long we've forgotten it even exists, let alone how to use it.

There, is however, another trigger that sometimes leads to archetypal awakening, namely crisis. In his therapy practice, Jung noticed that often, his patients would start dreaming of circles when they were in danger of succumbing to psychosis. Their psyche, he understood, was reaching for a medicine that could restore their mental health.

In fact, it was through a serious crisis of his own that Jung first discovered the healing power of the circle. In 1913, at the age of 38, he experienced a serious mental breakdown during which he was haunted by troubling visions and inner voices. Later, he said that during this period, he felt "menaced by a psychosis." Visions assaulted him incessantly, which he compared to rocks falling on his head, thunderstorms and molten lava. "I often had to cling to the table," he recalled, "so as not to fall apart."[5]

Desperate for relief, Jung started drawing and painting mandalas on a daily basis. In his autobiography, he wrote, "I sketched every morning in a notebook a small circular drawing, a mandala, which seemed to correspond to my inner situation at the time. With the help of these drawings I could observe my psychic transformations from day to day." If you've never seen Jung's mandalas, I highly recommend that you look them up. They are beautiful and may we ll inspire you to try your own hand at mandala painting.

Today, we might say that our entire world is in crisis; every day, we are bombarded by bad news. More and more people are feeling stressed, anxious, confused, and overwhelmed. Is it purely coincidental that suddenly, people are fascinated with crop circles and labyrinths, kaleidoscopes and stone circles? I don't think so. Our collective consciousness recognizes the circle as a medicine it needs.

The Role of Sacred Geometry in Circlework

Most circle gatherings pay no attention to sacred geometry. To some degree, the form still affects people. However, as long as the inner mandala lies dormant, the circle will only touch them from the outside and its transformative power will remain limited. But once the inner archetype awakens, our lives begin to restructure themselves from the inside out, often quite rapidly. Indeed, at times the process can feel overwhelmingly intense, stretching the upper limit of what we feel capable of handling. Yet this seems to be what our souls want and need at this time. "I am moving through layers of growth at lightning speed," a young woman told us. "It's painful. And yet, I have never felt this safe, this held."

If you are interested in using circle gatherings as a healing tool for yourself and your community, I recommend that you too pay close attention to their geometric form. For example, even while listening to a story or discussing an idea, try to remain conscious of the circle as the spiritual matrix that informs your work. Even while relating to other people, be mindful of the circle as a source of numinous power. In this way, you will learn to live in two worlds at once: Even as you're dealing with ordinary mundane concerns, you're also in touch with something greater.

One of the first things you might notice, were you to attend a Circlework retreat, is how carefully we tend to the shape of the circle. If all we cared about was that we could talk to each other, then a lopsided circle would do just fine. But if we want to create a true

VOICES FROM THE CIRCLE

In our dance, I suddenly saw circles upon circles upon circles. I felt the ancientness of what we are doing, and how it goes far beyond the personalities of those who happen to be present today. I saw our ancestors gathering in circles throughout the ages, and I realized that their circles are present with us in the room.

mandala, then form matters. It matters, for example, whether the candle in the center is *really* in the center. If it isn't, you'll experience a subtle yet noticeable sense of imbalance and tension. Not everyone will be consciously aware of this. Yet when finally, someone decides to push the candle over a few inches, a tiny sigh of relief will ripple through the circle.

Voices from the Circle

I love the image of the circle as a wheel with spokes that connect each person to the center. For me, it affirms that we are sparks of the greater source, and we are each valuable. That becomes the backdrop against which we can look at those voices that say, "I'm shit," or "I don't have what it takes," and we can recognize them as untruth. The fact that we each have that connection to the center tells us that we are of that realm, we are of the Spirit, we are infinite.

When we consciously connect with the power of sacred geometry, a hitherto locked door swings open, leading us out of ordinary into sacred space. We might also call it ritual space, for the mere act of consciously forming a circle is in itself a sacred ritual that has the power to transport the psyche and awaken the soul.

By honoring the circle as a divine thought form, we awaken to the spiritual matrix that informs our work. We acknowledge, as we step into the circle, that what happens here is of another order than what goes on in daily life. We are sitting in a circle, not just for the sake of convenience, so that everyone can see everyone else, but because the circle connects us to the realm of the sacred.

To form a simple mandala, all you need is a center and a circumference. Using just these two geometric elements, you can invoke the sacred presence. In Circlework, however, we work with a total of six geometric elements: the center, the circumference, the four directions, the spokes of the wheel, the Heaven-Earth axis and the Axis Mundi. Each of these six elements is not only an essential part of the mandala, but also a teacher and guide in its own right. Each has its own unique gifts and powers and supports our work in different ways.

Here's a brief overview over the six elements and their significance. For more detailed information on the significance of each element and how to tap its special gifts, please refer to the *Circlework Training Manual*.

1 The Center. The center symbolizes God, Spirit, the womb, the source, the One. Working with the center evokes the experience of being centered in ourselves and connected to our spiritual source.

2 The Four Directions. Radiating out from the center, the four directions define the co-ordinates of sacred space. They represent our interconnectedness with all beings, past, present and future, the principle of manifestation and the practice of living with reverence for nature.

3 The Circumference: The circumference represents connection, community, acceptance, compassion, listening, witnessing, love, holding, nurturance, mothering, boundaries and protection. It evokes the experience of feeling intimately connected with others and completely accepted for who we are.

4 The Spokes of the Wheel: The spokes of the wheel represent our path, our journey, our calling, purpose and direction. Working with them evokes a sense of respect and gratitude for the unique path each one of us walks as we approach the center, and as we carry the gifts of the center back out into our world.

5 The Heaven-Earth Axis: The Heaven-Earth axis represents courage, individuality, authority, authenticity, power, voice, visibility, uniqueness, diversity, integrity, confidence and self-respect. Working with this dimension connects us with our own internal power. (Please see Chapter 8 for a more in-depth discussion of the Heaven-Earth axis.)

6 The Axis Mundi (literally "world axis"): Just as the heaven-earth axis runs through the center of our body, so the Axis Mundi runs vertically through the center of the circle. It represents our access to other realms of being and other states of consciousness.

VOICES FROM THE CIRCLE

I love the image of the circle as a wheel with spokes that connect each person to the center. For me, it affirms that we are sparks of the greater source, and we are each valuable. That becomes the backdrop against which we can look at those voices that say, "I'm shit," or "I don't have what it takes," and we can recognize them as untruth. The fact that we each have that connection to the center tells us that we are of that realm, we are of the Spirit, we are infinite.

Symptoms of Archetypal Awakening

How do we know when the mandala has come alive within our psyche? One symptom to watch for are circle dreams. After she started practicing Circlework, a young African American woman called Fiona started having recurrent dreams about circles. In these dreams, the circle wasn't just a geometric form. Rather, it was a signpost guiding her home to herself:

> For most of my life, I felt that I didn't have a clue who I was. But since joining this circle, I've been experiencing an awakening. I feel my ancestors with me. I dream about the circle all the time. Circles have been going on for a long time and I know it; I have been part of them. In my dreams, I'm part of a circle and I know who I am.

Even reading this book may cause you to start dreaming about circles. If you do, take notice—such dreams are precious gifts.

Yet dreams are not the only symptom of archetypal awakening. By far the most common sign is a radical shift in perception. As long as the archetype lies dormant, all we see, when we look at a circle, is the familiar geometric shape. But once the archetype awakens, the circle comes alive in a whole new way. Suddenly, we perceive it as a living guide who is waiting to take us by the hand and lead us where we want to go. The circle, we realize, is a living being, a field of sacred intelligence that can talk to us and share its secrets.

Many years ago, my friend Alyssa experienced the spontaneous awakening of the circle archetype during a movement practice. To this day, she still counts this among the peak experiences of her life. Here's her account of what happened.

> We did an exercise where we all spread out in the room and moved to music, just paying attention to whatever came up in us. Eventually, we were supposed to come back and stand together in a circle.

As I was moving from my own space back to the group, I had this sudden clarity that in this moment, I was taking my place in the circle, and that really, that was what my life was all about. I understood that on this earth, there is a circle, and everyone here has a place in it, and my place was waiting for me. All I had to do was stand in it. I didn't have to be in the center, and I didn't have to take care of anyone else in the circle.

I will never forget this experience. I had often felt that if I wasn't special in some way, either because I was the person everyone relied on, or because I was the center of attention, then I would be invisible and insignificant. But in this moment, I realized that I could be special and unique, without being the center of attention or separating myself from others. It was so humbling, in a positive way, and it gave me such an incredible feeling of compassion and universality and connection to everybody else. There was a sense of relief, too, because I saw that all I really needed to do was to be me and to take my rightful place in the circle.

From this moment on, Alyssa knew, in an entirely new way, that her worth did not depend on being special or making an extraordinary contribution. Contrary to what her ego had been telling her, she didn't need to earn her place in the world. Instead of struggling to prove herself, she could relax into the knowledge that she, like all of Earth's children, was beautiful, sacred and unique. She was enough, just the way she was.

In my circles, I've often witnessed the sudden awakening of the circle archetype. Tanya, for example, knew nothing about sacred geometry or archetypes. Nonetheless, during a guided meditation, the circle archetype sprang to life in her in ways that changed her life forever. Here's what she experienced:

First, I saw us forming a circle of light. Everyone here was part of it, but it was more abstract than bodies. It looked like a disk or

Voices from the Circle

I love calling in the directions. Something happens when we do that; I feel a very strong sense of presence. I've started doing it every morning and it totally changes the energy with which I move into the day.

a wheel, with a center and many spokes. Actually, it looked like a space ship, like a UFO. It was bright white, and it emitted very powerful, radiant light. As soon as I got the image, it tilted, like a spaceship in motion, and I saw it was moving. It wasn't static at all but extremely dynamic. And I knew without a doubt that I was here to learn about that power. Then the space ship became a circle of people again, and I saw an image of myself. My heart was glowing, and I was holding a bowl out of which this lovely light came spiraling down, sparkling in all the rainbow colors. It was beautiful and it felt like such a blessing. And then, the circle spoke to me. There weren't many words, but it told me to love myself and have compassion for myself.

Just as you would nurture a new love by spending time with your sweetheart, so your relationship with the circle, too, will grow stronger if you give it your full attention. This is not hard to do. After all, circles surround you on all sides. Chances are, if you look up right now, you'll see at least one, perhaps even many—a round glass or plate, the wheels on your child's toy truck, the ring on your finger.

To connect with the circle as an inner resource and teacher is a great blessing. Whether you paint circles, build stone labyrinths or gather in circles—to the extent that you focus on sacred geometry, the mandala will come alive within the very core of your being to support your healing and awakening.

Start thinking of the circle not just as a geometric form, but as a friend and teacher. Develop a habit of paying attention to the circles that surround you. I promise you that if you consistently invite the circle to connect with you, it eventually will.

It's a relationship well worth cultivating, for when you get lost, the circle can guide you home. When you forget who you are, it can remind you. When you feel unworthy, it can connect you to the source of love within. Wherever you go, it will go with you, like an umbilical cord linking you to your divine source.

Listening to the Circle

The following exercise is an example of one the foundational practices we use in Circlework. It's called "I Am Writing," and it's based on the premise that everything has a voice. Stones have a voice, trees and animals have a voice, the soul has a voice. *I Am Writing* helps us tune into those voices so we can connect more deeply with ourselves and our world.

Sit down with pen and paper, and open to the possibility that the circle might have an intelligence, a will, and a voice that can speak to you. Set the intention that for the next few minutes, you will listen and write down whatever it might say. Begin by communicating your willingness to listen to the circle by writing down the words:

> *I am the circle.*

Now, just listen for the voice of the circle. Listen with total focus, as if you were trying to hear the distant call of a bird in the forest. Eventually, words may start bubbling up. Sometimes, it might be just a single phrase. Other time, words will come rushing out faster than you can write. Either way, note down whatever shows up. If you see images or colors, make a note of them, too.

Don't push or try to "think up" something. If nothing happens, let that be okay too. Remember that this practice is more about receptivity than activity, more about listening than thinking.

Write down whatever emerges without editing, censoring, or questioning. If your mind begins to wander, gently come back to your breath, to the present moment, and to your intention of listening to the circle.

Is what you're writing just the product of your imagination?

Best not to worry about it. Instead, approach this practice as creative play. Of course, you *are* using your imagination. But then, imagination is always one of the main channels through which insight flows. So just stay open and welcome whatever comes. If the results prove useful, great. If not, you can discard them. Set your critical mind aside for now.

For more suggestions on how to use *I am Writing*, please refer to the *Circlework Training Manual*.

CHAPTER 4

THE EVOLUTION OF PLANETARY CIRCLES

You and I are the force for transformation in the world. We are
the consciousness that will define the nature of the reality we are
moving into.
                    Ram Dass

The practice of gathering in circles is one of the oldest on earth, dating back eons. However, it would be a mistake to assume that in our circles today, we're simply picking up where our ancestors left off. Despite the similarities between our circles and those of tribal peoples, there are also significant differences. To understand what they are, it's helpful to divide history into three stages:

◎ The Tribal Era

◎ The Era of Individualism

◎ The Global Era

The Tribal Era

The tribal era is by far the longest of the three stages, spanning millions of years. Throughout this period, virtually all humans lived in small tribal groups.

Culturally, tribes varied enormously. Still, most shared some important commonalities. For example, a tribe was usually a clearly demarked entity. Though in some cases intermarriage might occur, each tribe remained a separate (and often isolated) society. As a result, tribes tended to be highly homogenous, with everyone sharing the same race, lineage, language, culture, religion, values, and so on. Typically, members of a tribe looked alike, thought alike, and lived alike.

Based on what we know about still existing tribal cultures, it's clear that the vast majority of tribal peoples used circles in their cultural and spiritual practices. Many built round dwellings. Some painted circles on their bodies, others danced and prayed and worshipped in circles. To this day, the circle is the standard format for tribal gatherings.

Imagine, for a moment, that you could jump back in time five thousand years. You come upon a tribe that has gathered in a circle to celebrate an important occasion. Everyone is present, from the tiniest baby to the oldest grandmother. Everyone knows each other—has known each other forever, and will presumably be together till the end of their days.

Watching these people, you realize that for them, their tribe and their circle are one and the same—the two are completely synonymous. Looking around the circle, they see the faces of their extended family. The circle protects and supports them, as a nest supports a clutch of eggs. It gives them not only their life, but also their identity, purpose and sense of self-worth.

Obviously, this is a far cry from where we stand today. We too might gather in circles to strengthen ourselves and our communities. However, we don't inherit our circles at birth. Rather we might choose to join a circle (or several), often for a limited period of time. The members of our circles aren't necessarily friends or members of our immediate family. They might not even share our race, religion, political beliefs or nationality.

For our ancestors, there was no life outside of their tribal circle. For us, there is. We can no longer depend on our circles for unconditional support, the way our ancestors could. Yet neither are we trapped in a web of absolute dependence. We might gain a lot of strength and support from our circles, but we are also free to leave at any time. True, we've lost that precious sense of knowing exactly where we belong and who our people are. On the other hand, we've gained an immense amount of freedom and independence.

Be that as it may, many women I work with still dream of that older, more nature-based world, and miss it terribly. Despite all the conveniences of modern life, they pine for that other way of life, where their community was there for them, every step of the way, where loneliness was unknown and no one fell through the cracks. Some tell me that in their eyes, the demise of the tribal era was nothing but a tragedy. If they could, they would gladly turn back the clock.

I understand their feelings. At the same time, I don't think we should view the demise of the tribal way of life as nothing but a tragic loss. From one angle, it most certainly is that. But seen in another way, might there be a more hopeful way of viewing our collective story? Instead of dismissing industrial society as a terrible mistake that should never have happened, might we recognize it as a difficult yet temporary transition into an entirely new way of living on planet Earth?

To answer that question, let's take a moment to consider how the transition from the first stage (the tribal era) to the third stage (the global era) unfolded.

The Second Stage: The Era of Individualism

The late Middle Ages were a time of turbulent and often violent change. Colonialism was on the rise, and its proponents were ruthless in their quest for power and wealth. Wherever they landed, their arrival spelled disaster for all indigenous cultures and their circle-based customs, rituals and ceremonies. Forced out of their round dwellings into square structures, the Native peoples of North America saw clearly that their entire way of life, with its exquisite attunement to the cycles of nature, was being destroyed.

Meanwhile, the indigenous traditions of Europe fared no better. For centuries, the Church had waged a war on what we now call Paganism, but what really comprised a wide range of indigenous spiritual practices. As we'll see in Chapter 6, one tradition that the Church was especially intent on eradicating were women's circles. All over Europe, women would congregate at certain times of the year, especially on solstices and equinoxes, to work their magic and celebrate their mysteries.

However, what ultimately led to the extinction of many forms of Pagan practice in Europe was the industrial revolution. Large cities sprang up, promising employment and drawing people like magnets from their rural homes towards urban centers of production. Here, the old tribal ways had no place. Instead of following the cyclical rhythms of sun and moon, plants and animals, people now had to adjust to the inorganic rhythms of machines.

VOICES FROM THE CIRCLE

My parents came from a time when the tribal circle had broken down, but the movement towards a new form of circle had not yet begun. So they had no circles of any kind. They had no communal home and no place to heal themselves. In some sense, they were really lost. It gives me chills to think about it.

By the 19th century, the circle had definitively lost its place at the center of European communal life. No longer did people gather in circles to celebrate, worship and pray. In schools, universities and churches, everyone sat in rows, all faces turned to the authority figures up front. Instead of dancing in circles, people danced in couples, cheek to cheek. The era of individualism had dawned, and the pursuit of communal unity ceded to that of personal happiness.

But looks are deceiving. On the one hand, there's no denying the tragic loss of countless circle-based customs and traditions—a loss that is ongoing, even today. Yet in another sense, the circle merely shape-shifted. Like a creature getting ready to hibernate, it went underground.

For even as the old communal circles disintegrated, the circle simultaneously began to emerge as a powerful symbol of individual wholeness. During the tribal era, a solitary individual had little worth. The tribe was the mandala that mattered; within it, the individual was a mere speck. People depended on tribal authorities and institutions to tell them who they were, what to believe and how to behave.

Now, with the industrial revolution, the basic unit of human whole-ness shifted to the individual. People began to consider that they might be intrinsically valuable, simply by virtue of being unique indi-viduals. "We too are mandalas," they proudly proclaimed. "The center, the universal source, lies within each one of us."

Consider, for example, the mystical poetry of the 13th-century Flemish nun Hadewijch II. In her words, we see this new awareness of the circle, not as an outer form but rather an inner mystery:

> Tighten
> to nothing
> the circle
> that is
> the world's things
> Then the Naked
> circle
> can grow wide,
> enlarging,
> embracing all.[1]

Hadewijch's words celebrate a new spirit of individual indepen-dence. Flying in the face of Church doctrine, she declares in no uncer-tain terms that she needs no religious authorities to mediate between herself and God. Having discovered the naked circle within, she knows Spirit as an inner presence with which she stands in intimate communion.

In this, Hadewijch is by no means alone. A surge of mystical expe-rience sweeps across Europe, the Middle East, and Asia. In unprece-dented numbers, men and women encounter God, not as an outer authority figure but as an inner presence. What better image to cap-ture the all-encompassing nature of this presence than the circle? Speaking of God as the Beloved, the 14th-century Persian poet Hafiz remarks:

I see the beautiful curve of a pregnant belly
Shaped by a soul within,
And the Earth itself,
And the planets and the Spheres—
I have gotten the hint:
There is something about circles
The Beloved likes.[2]

For thousands of years, people lived in a state of near total dependence on their tribe. From it, they derived their sense of identity, their self, their value. But in the late Middle Ages, a new sense of individual power emerges. Like wildfire, a new awareness spreads: "We can access the Source within. We don't need others to make us whole; our wholeness comes from within." Ordinary people begin to demand their right to self-determination. Authority, they declare, is not something reserved for kings and popes: The true source of authority lies within. Out of this realization, democracy is born.

Individualism unleashes an explosion of creativity, ingenuity and inventiveness. Besides triggering waves of mystical fervor, religious rebellion and political unrest, it also inspires a new fascination with human consciousness. Modern psychology evolves, along with countless new methods for approaching specific mental problems. What is it that makes us tick? How does the psyche function? What mechanisms is it governed by? The exploration of these and other questions has immensely deepened our psychological understanding and has spawned an astounding array of new tools and techniques designed to help us cultivate our inner center.

One of the pioneers in this process was C.G. Jung, who dedicated his life work to the journey of individuation. As we mentioned previously, he was one of the first modern Westerners to recognize the power of the circle and invite it back into mainstream awareness. But Jung was also a died-in-the-wool individualist, firmly rooted in second stage thinking. Though he recognized the unifying power of the circle, he never facilitated circle gatherings. Instead, he used the circle exclusively as a tool for individual healing.

The Dawn of the Global Era

Speak of the global era, and we usually think of the global economy or the Internet. But I would argue that these phenomena are secondary. The real mark of the global era is the emergence of a new consciousness that recognizes the oneness of planet Earth.

If the birthday of this new consciousness were a national holiday, it would be celebrated on July 20th, for it was on this day in 1969 that man first stepped onto the surface of the moon. That event was indeed, as Neil Armstrong triumphantly proclaimed, "a giant leap for mankind." What made it so, however, was not the fact that our species had arrived on the moon. No question, this was a great technological feat. But far more significant was the fact that, turning back towards Earth, the astronauts saw, for the first time, what our home planet looks like from space. That sight changed Neil Armstrong's life forever, and has profoundly affected the consciousness of most humans alive today.

In that moment, the era of individualism came to an end. Henceforth, the basic unit of human wholeness would no longer be the tribe or the individual, but rather Gaia, our beautiful blue-green planet. Earth is now our foundational mandala, the sacred orb we live and depend on. Of course, we still have our tribal affiliations. We still want personal happiness and fulfillment. Yet we know, in a whole new way, that Earth is one, and that we belong to a single human family, a single planetary mandala, and a single interconnected web.

Now, our foremost task is to align our consciousness with that greater truth. For millennia, we viewed Earth as all-powerful and infinitely vast. Today, we know that we live on a small planet, members of a global family that will either learn to live together in peace or perish. No longer can we justify reserving our love and concern for members of our immediate tribe. Instead, we need to cultivate a more inclusive kind of love that embraces all members of our extended family, for upon their well-being and happiness depends our own.

This, then, is the pivotal realization that informs all third stage circles. Third stage circles don't negate or dismiss the goals of previous stages. We too want our families, communities and nations to be vital and strong. We too want to thrive and prosper as individuals. But we see clearly that everything we strive for is predicated on the health of Gaia, our planet, and that within her body, we are all interconnected.

This is by no means a new insight—Buddhist texts written two thousand years ago already portrayed the cosmos as a vast interconnected web. Yet for thousands of years, interconnection remained a highly esoteric concept that didn't appear to have much practical relevance. Today, on the other hand, our interconnectedness is arguably the most important truth we need to embrace.

The global economy, the Internet, the new discoveries that have revolutionized subatomic physics—all these have given new meaning to the concept of interconnection. But what has really bumped our interconnectedness to the top of the list of truths we can't afford to ignore is the environmental crisis. The weather, nuclear fallout, pollution—they have no regard for national boundaries.

Be conscious, says Vietnamese peace activist Thich Nhat Hanh, of the trees that your daily newspaper is made of. Be conscious of the clouds that nourished those trees. Be mindful of the web that sustains us, lest we destroy it. To save our planet, we need to perceive it as it is: A single, interconnected organism.

If you're reading this book, you are probably well aware of interconnection as an essential key to understanding our world. Still, the kind of mindfulness that Thich Nhat Hanh recommends doesn't come easy to us. Our ancestors never had to consider whether their shoes had been made by slave laborers in China. They didn't have to wonder where and under what conditions their food had been grown, or what

VOICES FROM THE CIRCLE

When I was in my twenties I joined a cult. My parents were absolutely appalled. But I was scared, and I was looking for a tribe to give me shelter and protect me. Things got pretty dark for a while, and by the time I got out of the cult, I was a mess. I had to do a lot of therapy, a lot of second stage work to find out who I really was. Now, I have friends and community who are really good for me. And thank God for my women's circle. They love me, but they also keep me on my toes and challenge me to get my shit together.

to do about global warming. To ask such questions, and to consider the entire planetary community in our daily decision-making—this is not something we do naturally or automatically. We're capable of it, for sure, but it takes practice and clear intention.

Third stage circles can go a long way towards helping us cultivate this new, more expansive type of awareness. Every third stage circle, no matter how small, views itself as a microcosm of the world, and its work as a contribution to the welfare of the entire planetary community. Its members understand how the mandala of their individual life intersects with the greater circle of their community, their world and their cosmos.

Circlework and the Awareness of Interconnection

In third stage circles, the awareness of our interconnectedness is a constant presence that profoundly impacts our work together. Because we are interconnected . . .

◎ Our lives are interwoven with those of all beings around the world.

◎ Our lives are interwoven with those of all beings past, present and future. We are connected to our ancestors and to the beings of the future.

◎ We are mirrors and teachers to each other. One person's breakthrough supports another.

◎ What we do matters. Our happiness matters. Our suffering matters. Our enlightenment matters. Our choices matter.

◎ Both the light and beauty and the darkness and evil we see in others are part of our own potential.

◎ Our own evolution contributes to the evolution of humankind.

Why We Need Second Stage Support

We, just like our tribal ancestors, must find ways to join forces, unite, and realize our oneness. Yet our circles, unlike theirs, tend to be extremely diverse. Often, we're trying to connect across all sorts of religious and cultural barriers, with people who may not share our background, our values or even our language. Moreover, we're dealing with all kinds of difficult and complex issues that didn't even exist a century ago. What this means is that we need vastly more sophisticated relational skills than previous generations did.

Thank God for everything we learned during the second stage! Individualism has given us permission to turn within, explore our inner terrain and plumb the depths of our consciousness. Besides helping us better understand how our psyche works, it has given us a wide array of transformational tools, from Focusing and Active Imagination to Gestalt therapy and Neurolinguistic Programming – to name just a few. When we hit an impasse in our circles, such tools can help us move through.

In hindsight, it almost looks like we were being prepared for what lies ahead. Like mountain climbers getting ready to scale the Himalayas, we've been outfitted with cutting-edge interpersonal skills, tools and concepts.

Unfortunately, mainstream society is just beginning to wake up to the crucial importance of disseminating psychological skills. It has yet to recognize the crucial importance of what I call "relational education" and to understand how much hinges on providing it to young and old alike.

Typically, however, Circlework tends to attract women who *do* recognize the importance and value of relational education. They've experienced different forms of psychotherapy and are trained in various healing modalities. They understand that every peace worker also needs to be a student of relational education, because relationships are where both war and peace begin.

At the same time, they are also keenly aware of the limitations that plague many schools of psychology. Today, modern psychology is only just beginning to integrate third stage awareness. Because it evolved in the era of individualism, it teaches us to view our thoughts and emotions as something very private, very personal. We are encouraged to assume that "These are my issues. They're related to my personal psychology, and I'm the one that's going to have to deal with them."

But this is at best a partial truth, because it doesn't take our hologrammatic nature into account. In a world of interconnection, nothing really belongs to one person alone. We are constantly mirroring back and forth aspects of the collective psyche.

Circlework helps us move beyond the excessive individualism of modern psychology. Every circle is, in our eyes, a microcosmic reflection of the world. Therefore we always ask ourselves: How does what is happening in the circle right now relate to what is happening in the world at large?

When we express our deepest truths in the circle, something happens that rarely happens in the privacy of our homes or in a psychotherapist's office. "My" emotional energy is honored as something that belongs to all of us, and that we can transform and heal together.

One of the great benefits of realizing our interconnectedness is that it can give us the courage to embrace our own transformation. Imagine, for example, a woman who is struggling with memories of sexual abuse. Her process may be difficult and painful. But to the extent that she feels herself connected to millions of other women worldwide who are struggling with the same issue, she will feel a deepened sense of purpose. She knows that her healing will benefit them too. This awareness instills in her a sense of commitment to something greater than herself. As she embarks on her healing journey, she is inspired, both by her desire for personal wholeness and her desire to contribute to the healing of others.

VOICES FROM THE CIRCLE

I've been in many second stage circles. But Circlework is different. I've grown so much, and yet there's a clear awareness that it's not about us me personally. We're sharing a collective journey, we're in this together, not just as a circle but as a species. For me, that has been so liberating. It's helped cut through the sense of shame and isolation I used to feel. I'm much more willing to speak out about things I care about. I used to feel like I didn't have the right to say what I thought until I had improved myself and become more enlightened. Now I know that we all have a contribution to make, and the time is now.

Four Kinds of Circles

Though we have entered the global era, most circles you'll come across are not third stage or planetary circles. Rather, they fall into one of four categories.

1 **First Stage Circles:** Authentic tribal circles are increasingly rare, but they do exist. Examples include Native American circles, African tribal circles, the circles of the Australian aboriginal peoples and many more.

2 **Second stage circles:** These focus primarily on personal benefits. For example, their aim might be to help people explore their psyche, heal emotional wounds or reclaim a sense of personal wholeness. Most women's support groups and therapeutically oriented groups are second stage circles, as are many spiritual groups. Second stage circles complement the work of third stage circles and fulfill an important need in our world.

3 **Third stage circles:** Third stage circle are still quite rare. They usually incorporate some elements of first stage circles and they also make use of second stage techniques. However, tribal or personal wholeness is never their ultimate goal. Rather, their purpose is to help us become mature, empowered planetary citizens. Consecrated to the well-being of the entire global community, they celebrate the diversity that is the hallmark of the global era.

4 **Pseudo-tribal circles:** Pseudo-tribal circles are not really tribal at all. Rather, they are a regressive phenomenon in which people try to artificially recreate the homogeneity of a tribal circle. Pseudo-tribal circles seduce their members by promising a strong sense of purpose and belonging. However, the price is exorbitant, including the sacrifice of one's autonomy and personal integrity. One example of a pseudo-tribal circle is the Ku Klux Klan, the ultra-racist organization responsible for countless acts of terror against black people.

We Need the Circle

Considering that the third stage of the circle has only just begun, it's all the more remarkable how quickly our relationship to circle gatherings has been transforming. A mere fifty years ago, they were routinely dismissed as one of the weird things that hippies did. Today, you'll find circles in churches and community centers, book clubs and AA meetings, drumming circles and therapy groups. Circles are back for a very simple reason: we need them. In these times of turbulence, transition and transformation, we simply cannot do without the resources of courage, wisdom and strength they give us access to.

Our world is at present drowning in negativity, violence, hatred, nastiness, pettiness and vindictiveness. In our circles, on the other hand, we share the goal of co-creating a space that we truly enjoy, a small yet potent pod of goodness that heals, nurtures and supports us. From here, peace, forgiveness and compassion radiate out into the world, touching countless others.

Imagine, for a moment, a peaceful global civilization. Utopian? Yes and no. In terms of technology and resources, it's totally doable. Moreover, I suspect at least 90 percent of humanity would love to see it happen. The real obstacles are, as is so often the case, not external but internal. This is why I view the deep inner work we do in the circle as an essential contribution to the healing of our world.

Will our species survive its own ignorance? Nobody can say. But if we do, it will be because sufficient numbers of people have embraced the task of creating a peaceful global civilization. Circlework is dedicated to supporting this process. Taking the gifts of our tribal ancestors as well as those of the modern era, we are weaving them into something entirely new—a way of being together that meets our needs as citizens of the 21st century.

VOICES FROM THE CIRCLE

In my family, I never felt a sense of belonging. I wanted a tribe, but they couldn't be that for me. Eventually I joined a therapy group. Really, it was a circle. For two years, we did a lot of healing together, a lot of second stage work. But then it ended, and now, I'm really yearning for community. I so love what we're doing here, in this circle. But I'm also worried, because where I live, there's nothing like this, nothing at all. What am I going to do?

Tribal Echoes

Grab your journal and a pen.

I'd like to invite you to spend a few minutes writing about your first stage experiences.

Well, you might say, I don't have any. I'm not a tribal person.

But the tribal era is not just a historical phase. It's also a layer within our individual and collective consciousness that has a lasting impact on how we think, feel, relate and behave.

If you think of your psyche as an archeological site, then the surface layers reflect your personal experience and history. As you dig deeper, you'll discover forms of conditioning that you inherited from your parents or ancestors, including some that evolved thousands, even hundreds of thousands of years ago. The tribal era may be over, but it still impacts you in the form of strong instinctual urges that nudge you this way or that.

Another point to consider is that when you were little, you relived the tribal era, without even realizing it. By that, I mean that you were born into a specific family with its own culture, myths and beliefs. It was a tribe of sorts, and since your very survival depended on having its support, you naturally tried to embrace the values it instilled in you.

For example, one of my friends grew up in a family where outsiders were never supposed to know what was really going on. The unspoken message was, "It's us against them. We have to hold together, and never let them see our vulnerability." These were the tribal rules he'd internalized.

VOICES FROM THE CIRCLE

Circlework has huge potential to heal the planet. Our separateness actually disappears before our eyes. It's a mode of being together where our commonality and our appreciation of each other is in the forefront, and our distances and judgments recede. If we could bring even 10% more of that into the world, our world would be transformed.

But your family is not the only place you may have encountered tribal consciousness. Maybe you were black and your family moved to a white neighborhood where you were made to feel less than welcome. Maybe you joined a religious or political group that felt like a tribe. Or maybe you live in a country that still has a strongly tribal flavor.

We no longer live in a tribal world. Nonetheless, in some individuals, the need for a sense of tribal belonging can become so strong that it drives them into the arms of cults, gangs, and even terrorist organizations. Even if you aren't that person, chances are, you know someone whose unconscious longing for a tribe led them to make unwise choices.

Spend a few minutes considering where first stage consciousness has touched your life. Then, pick one of your memories and spend ten minutes writing about it. What gifts did the experience offer you? What challenges did it pose? How did it change you?

CHAPTER 5

INVOKING THE SACRED FEMININE

In my mind, Spirit is still male. I'm feeling tears welling up because of my longing to connect with the feminine. In my family, my mother was weak and my father was omnipotent. I never realized how I was projecting my parents onto the image of God. This morning, when we did the exercise of writing to God, I intentionally changed the gender and wrote to Her instead of Him.

Nothing ignites our passion the way relationship does. We're wired for it; it's what gives our lives meaning and purpose.

In the realm of spirituality, the same holds true. We need to feel that Spirit is not just an abstract idea but our personal friend, lover, teacher, child or parent. Without that sense of connection, our heart won't open and we won't experience the passion that can fuse two into one. We need to feel, not just in touch with Spirit, but connected in the deepest, most intimate ways.

To facilitate this sense of connection, people have always envisioned Spirit in human forms, both male and female. Of course there are some who actually believe in God's maleness or femaleness. But these days, most of us recognize the naiveté of such beliefs. Whatever Spirit might be, clearly it transcends gender.

Nonetheless, it can be helpful to work with human images. For though Spirit transcends gender, we ourselves do not. We relate differently to men and women, and have different sets of feelings and issues towards each sex. Pairing the concept of divinity with male images unlocks different chambers in our psyche than pairing it with female ones. The thought of a divine Father calls forth different emotions than that of a divine Mother.

Why do we make images of the Divine? One answer is that we need a focal point for our devotion. Another is that we need mirrors that reflect our own highest potential. We need to be reminded that even though we might be damaged and flawed, we're also mysterious and infinitely beautiful.

In our culture, many of us struggle to find the spiritual mirrors we need. This is true of men and women alike, though for different reasons. For men, the problem is that traditional images of God tend to be distorted by patriarchal bias. Therefore, they often fail to reflect men's authentic nature. For women, the wholesale absence of feminine images can pose a serious obstacle to realizing their own divinity.

As long as we view ourselves exclusively as human beings, we can't really know who we are. To develop a healthy sense of pride and self-respect, we need to experience ourselves as embodiments of divinity. Without that direct, intimate realization of our own sacredness, we are bound to depend on others for validation. When that outer validation is not forthcoming, we're likely to feel hollow and insignificant. Naturally, this leaves us more inclined to betray ourselves in order to gain the validation we crave. When we get it, our ego may feel temporarily strong and vibrant. But eventually, those feelings fade and we look for another "fix."

Fortunately, at this crucial time in history, we've finally reached a point where we can choose to shed the husks of outdated patriarchal beliefs in order to rediscover and remember both the sacred feminine and the sacred masculine.

Voices from the Circle

Today is the anniversary of my mother's death. I've always felt like I wasn't loving enough to her, that I should have done more for her when she was dying. But in our meditation, I heard her saying, "I'm here with you, I love you." My immediate reaction was, how could she love me? But I'm feeling it. I feel her enveloping me, surrounding me with tenderness. I'm just overwhelmed by her love. I can't stop crying. My tears . . . Being unable to control them is so rare for me. I didn't even know I was carrying that weight of guilt. But now I realize it was there, and it has lifted. I'm finally forgiving myself. I am free.

The Sacred

What exactly do we mean, when we describe the masculine or the feminine as "sacred?"

To answer that question, we first need to understand that we use the word "sacred" in two very different ways. One is what we might would call the religious way. In religion, sacredness is usually presented as a static quality that certain objects or people possess. For example, in Islam, the Kaaba is sacred. It isn't sometimes sacred and sometimes not. Rather, its sacredness is immutable.

However, we often use the word "sacred" in a far more subjective way. Imagine two friends watching the same sunset. The sunset isn't intrinsically sacred, but one friend might experience it as so, while the other does not. Similarly, one woman might describe giving birth as the most sacred experience of her life, while another recalls it being pure torture. So this second kind of sacredness depends less on the object of our perception and more on our own state of consciousness.

When I speak of the sacred feminine, I'm using the word in this second sense. Can we look at women, and at feminine images, and recognize the sacred presence within them?

Most of the time, the answer is no, we can't. Our vision is so clouded by social conditioning that all we see is the extent to which a woman conforms to collective standards of youth and beauty. Still, there are moments in which those blinders fall away and our perception shifts abruptly, revealing the presence of the sacred feminine.

I think, for example, of an experience I had when I was teaching at a summer camp where over 300 women had gathered for a week of sacred play. On the last morning of our time together, I witnessed an amazing scene.

Try to picture, if you will, a large, beautiful lake at dawn. Imagine mist rising over the waters, obscuring the dark woods on the other side. It's very quiet. All you can hear are the sounds of birds awakening.

And then, you hear a drumbeat, slow and steady.

And suddenly, groups of women begin to appear. All are totally silent. All are naked. Slowly, in silence, they begin to wade into the water. More keep coming, wave upon wave of women's bodies, young and old, women of all shapes and sizes, pouring into the lake to offer silent prayers for the world.

Under normal circumstances, I'm sure my mind would have instantly flashed its well-rehearsed judgments: That woman is fat, that one is thin, she is beautiful, she is not. But that morning, all that mental babble was utterly and completely absent. The scene was so ancient, so primordial that it silenced my mind and transported me back to a time long before such notions ever existed. What I saw, as I looked out across the lake, weren't separate women wading into the water. It was the sacred feminine herself, in all her different forms.

The beauty of the experience was overwhelming. I started to cry, not with sadness, but with a profound sense of wonder, reverence and awe.

In our world, that kind of event is rare indeed. Still, it can happen. In my circles, I've witnessed many such moments in which women awakened to their own sacredness. What might it be like to live in a society where this was our normal way of perceiving women? What would our world look like, if we all knew ourselves as sacred beings?

At present, our near universal lack of reverence for the sacred feminine is one of the main causes of violence and warfare on our planet. Not by coincidence are so many war zones also places where women are oppressed and the sacred feminine is dishonored.

The Feminine

The fog of confusion that surrounds the word "sacred" becomes even thicker when we turn to the word "feminine." What the heck does that mean, anyway?

The problem is that as compulsive head-thinkers, we keep trying to grasp the essence of the feminine through the rational, analytic mind. For example, we make lists of attributes that we consider masculine or feminine. The feminine is compassionate and gentle, we say. She is protective and nurturing.

But is this true? Or are we merely parroting old gender stereotypes?

Of course, it's important to understand those stereotypes, because they're part of the conditioning we've all internalized. Why do we tend to equate softness and vulnerability with weakness? Why do so many men amputate big chunks of who they are in order to avoid appearing "soft?" Knowing that certain qualities are traditionally considered feminine can help us recognize where our resistance to owning them comes from.

That said, traditional views of what is masculine or feminine don't actually tell us much about who we really are. Science claims there are differences between the male and the female brain, but what conclusions are we to draw from this? For eons, we've been arguing fiercely about the question of what is masculine and feminine, and still there's no consensus. After all, supposedly "feminine" traits can easily be found in most men, as well.

World mythology, too, thwarts our attempts to limit the sacred feminine to a narrow set of attributes and qualities. Some goddesses are gentle and compassionate, others are violent and wildly destructive. The only thing we can honestly say about them is that they are just as diverse as we ourselves are.

Unfortunately, many authors in the field of psychology and spirituality continue to reinforce the old gender stereotypes. For example, women are often encouraged to explore their "masculine side," men their "feminine side."

As I see it, this kind of terminology doesn't serve us well. What's the point of telling a man that his sensitivity is a feminine trait and therefore incongruous with his physical sex? Why suggest to a woman that her strength isn't really part of her feminine nature? Do we really want to teach our children that half of their psychological makeup belongs to the opposite sex? In my view, this will only reinforce their inner fragmentation. Better focus on giving them the support they need to manifest the full spectrum of their human potential.

The Goddess as Vibration

In Circlework, we don't approach the sacred feminine as a religious figure, nor do we view her as an amalgam of supposedly female virtues and qualities.

But then, what the heck is she?

To answer that question, we need to stop relying on words, and instead open to direct, non-conceptual experience. Imagine, for a moment, that some extraterrestrial visitors had arrived at your doorstep. Turns out, they're gourmets, and their mission is to sample all the delicious varieties of food we have here on Earth. Raspberries, for example. They've heard raspberries are amazing. So they want to know, "What do they taste like?"

"Well," you stammer. "Uh . . . They're sweet. At least when they're ripe."

You do your best, but no matter what you say, your guests just stare at you with blank eyes.

Finally, you jump up and excuse yourself for a minute. You rush to the nearest supermarket, from where you return with a basket of perfectly ripe raspberries. As your guests pop the plump berries into their mouths, their eyes light up with delight and comprehension. Raspberries! Oh! Now they understand.

Nobody would claim that raspberries aren't real. Nobody would say that if you can't adequately convey their flavor, then clearly, they don't exist.

Yet in regards to the sacred feminine and masculine, this is what we often do. They too are vibrational frequencies that can't be captured in words or concepts. Nonetheless they are absolutely real. And just like raspberries, they too can be known—not

Voices from the Circle

For years, I've been studying with Sufi teachers. I practice turning, the Whirling Dervish practice, and I love it. But I was having trouble with the patriarchal aspects of it. When I turn, I often smile because I feel such ecstasy. In my tradition, this is not okay. I was criticized and told there should be no sign of joy on the surface. I struggled with this for a long time. It just didn't feel right to me. All my life, I'd been trying to come out of hiding, and now they were telling me to hide once more. Circlework has so deepened my connection with the sacred feminine, and it has helped me find a solution I can live with. Now, I sometimes wear a white dress when I turn, instead of the Sufi garment. When I wear that white dress, it symbolizes that I am turning as the sacred feminine. I turn as a woman, wearing jewels and showing my smile. This process has been such a dance of invisibility and visibility. And the truth is, I love being visible. I love it so much! For me, hiding is not the answer. The light within me yearns to be acknowledged, celebrated, and expressed.

through the mind, but through direct personal experience.

Rituals, such as the one I described above, are one way of accessing that experience. Another is through circles. Circles, you see, are energetic amplifiers. Whatever energy we focus on in the circle becomes intensified a thousand fold. Just as a lens can start a fire by focusing many rays of sunlight onto one point, so circles can amplify specific vibrational frequencies.

VOICES FROM THE CIRCLE

In our circle, I got a strong image of just how bad the goddess wants to come through. She was flaming up in the center, undulating and beautiful. I was watching her, this incredible feminine energy. Then I felt her come up through my own spine too. I tone down my energy a lot. I've gotten a lot of flak for being big and having big energy. Now, I want to set myself free. I want to wear silk and jewels and take care of my body. I want to undulate and dance.

This is something our indigenous ancestors knew well. Most indigenous peoples had circle gatherings for men, others for women, and yet others for both sexes. They recognized that women's vibrational field is different than men's, and that in a circle of women, the essence of the feminine can be intensified to the point that everyone can feel it. Similarly, circles of men can amplify the energetic presence of the sacred masculine. Therefore, same-sex circles can serve as a powerful aid in awakening us to the essence of our own gender.

One of the reasons I feel so passionate about women's circles is because they connect us with the sacred feminine, both in ourselves and in other women. By helping us rediscover our own gender in a new way, they prepare us to move out into the world—not with the power of a man, but with the uniquely feminine power of a self-realized woman.

For a woman who has never experienced the sacred feminine in any meaningful way, or has always thought of God as male, such first-hand experiences of the sacred feminine can be life-changing. Consider the following exchange between myself and a young woman called Patricia. Patricia begins by expressing her sense of bewilderment. What is the sacred feminine?

I have a hard time accessing the sacred feminine. I was brought up with God being a male in the sky. My sense of God has expanded greatly, but I still haven't opened to the divine Feminine. Truthfully, I'm not sure what that is. It's not something I have any experience with.

Words, I know, will never address Patricia's confusion. So, instead of wasting time on futile explanations, I invite her to take a seat in the vortex of power and presence that is the center of our mandala.

J: Can you come and sit in the center for a minute?

(She does.)

I would invite you to feel the women around you for a moment. Like a sponge, let yourself absorb that field of energy. Feel how your body responds to it.

(Silence.)

P: The first thing that comes up is that my body isn't absorbing it. It's really hard for me.

(Silence.)

Oh, I feel it!

J: Can you sense the difference between the feminine energy that is here, and how it might feel if you were sitting in a circle of men?

P: Oh yes. Oh, yes.

J: And how does the feminine feel right now?

P: I feel totally nurtured and held and honored and respected and loved.

J: The divine feminine isn't sitting in the sky. She's sitting around you. Right now, this group of women is embodying the feminine energy for you, but it's not really personal. What you're feeling is the essence of the feminine spirit, the essence of the Mother.

Long silence.

J: Do you get a little hit of it?

P: Yes, oh yes, I'm feeling it so strongly now. Thank all of you.

I wish every woman could have the experience of basking in a field of sacred feminine energy. Similar, I wish that every man had the opportunity to consciously experience the beauty of the sacred masculine. Without connection to the essence of our own gender, how shall we know who we are? Disconnected from our own nature, how shall we maintain a healthy sense of pride? How shall men and women relate in joyful, loving and fulfilling ways, if they haven't connected with the very essence of their own sex?

Healing Our Mother Wounds

The divine Mother can feel so far away. And suddenly I see that she's right here, in all her glory, looking at me through your eyes.

When I lived in India, people would often say to me, "There is no more powerful love than that of a mother for her child. A mother's love is pure and unconditional."

I would just stare at them in silent disbelief. I knew all too many women who believed that their mothers had damaged them irreparably. To them, the word "mother" referred, not to a friend but to an enemy intent on criticizing them and putting them down. The last thing they would have said was that their mothers had given them unconditional love.

Maria, for example, is a young activist who had suffered severe sexual abuse at the hands of her mother. After telling her story in the circle, she added:

> I was abused by a woman, so sharing my story with women brings up feelings. I have never before talked about it the way I did today. It feels good, but also, I feel a little shaky. This is as vulnerable as I've ever been. So much happened to me when I was growing up that broke my bond with women. So for me, learning to trust women again is huge.

Maria is not alone. Even if we weren't abused, many of us had less than stellar moms. As a result, we may have a hard time opening up to other women, let alone to the image of a divine Mother.

But here's the good news: If we persist in welcoming Spirit in the form of pure, unconditional mother love, two things will happen. First, we'll receive a spiritual lifeline that will support us till the day we die. And second, our personal mother wounds will begin to heal. As our relationship to the divine Mother grows stronger and more solid, the shortcomings of our biological moms will be of less concern.

Eventually, we're able to forgive our mothers for being who they were. Equally importantly, we'll be able to forgive God for having paired us up with a flawed and disappointing human mother. Instead of blaming our mothers for the wounds we suffered, we'll find it easy to embrace whatever positive and valuable gifts they gave us.

Today, I understand what my Indian friends were trying to tell me, and I know they were absolutely right. Clearly, not all mothers are loving. Yet beyond our invariably flawed human mothers, we all have access to the Mother as an archetypal figure who lives within us all.

Who has not marveled at the incredible patience and tenderness with which most animal moms care for their young? Nobody has to give them lessons. The mother energy simply takes over and dictates their actions. Even the fiercest tigress becomes the very embodiment of gentleness with her cubs.

We were all born from a mother who was born from a mother who was born from a mother— a lineage of mothers reaching back millions of years. We had mothers long before we evolved into human form. Each one of them successfully managed to raise her child, guided by a force that curbed her natural selfishness and that, in many cases, truly did transform her into a vessel of unconditional love. How, then, could the image of mother as a source of life, nurturance, protection, and unconditional love not be firmly planted in our consciousness?

To invoke this archetypal mother, as we do in my circles, is not a religious act but rather an act of psychological healing. Her image connects us to a source of love that we do not have to earn, or work for but that simply is, like the devotion of a cat for her kittens. By opening to this primal, indestructible love, we learn how to unconditionally love and accept ourselves.

Voices from the Circle

During a meditation in the circle, I had an experience in which the sacred feminine appeared to me. I saw her very clearly, seated in my head above my right eye. Now, she is always there. She is wearing a rich, velvet-like garment with folds of light. She is made of light, she emanates light, she breathes light, and she lives in me. This is the holy Spirit, the Beloved. Before Circlework I never had an experience so close, so intimate. I feel she's there for me and hears me when I open myself and avail myself of her presence. In her presence I know that I am a lantern, a light, a gift. I am sufficient, I am enough.

Western psychology would have us believe that if we didn't receive the mother love we needed in childhood, we never will—the loss is permanent and irreversible. We can heal our wounds to some extent, but we'll forever bear the scars. This is, I believe, an unfortunate misconception that makes us feel powerless over our past, when in fact, we are not.

It's as if we were standing in front of an empty fridge and complaining that we're all out of milk. All the while, a cow with overflowing udders is standing patiently in our back yard. Yet if someone were to point her out, we'd say, "No, you're imagining things. That cow isn't real."

Yet in my experience, she's very real indeed. Many women I work with say she's appeared in their dreams to remind them of her presence and shake them awake. She holds up a mirror to their essential self and reconnects them with who they really are. One woman tells us:

Yesterday I dreamed that I was taking part in a ritual. Through imagery and movement I was guided to a space where I saw an image of a lovely face. As I was looking deeply into the eyes of this lovely being, she suddenly transformed into an intense, piercing, powerful reality. I knew she was the Mother and was held in the fierceness of her gaze.

Connection with the divine Mother can heal the inner child who never knew a mother's love, and can help us forgive our biological mothers for their shortcomings. Lana says that for her, this has been one of the most precious gifts of Circlework:

I am now a woman who has forgiven her mother. For me, this has been life-changing. Most of my deepest wounds have been in relationship to my mother. All the ways in which those wounds limited and distorted my presence in the world are now dissolving. I am more able to serve and love fully and to live in joy.

In our world, everything we associate with mothering—safety, protection, nourishment, love—is in short supply. Billions of people struggle to survive in harsh, inhospitable environments, besieged by violence and warfare, trauma and poverty. By opening to the mother archetype within us all, we empower ourselves to serve as healers to a world that is famished for the gentle touch of a mother. By aligning ourselves with her energy, we become conduits of a healing medicine that our world desperately needs.

Once a woman knows herself as a daughter and embodiment of the sacred feminine, she becomes a force to be reckoned with. Having awakened to her own sacredness, she also knows the sacredness of nature. And so, she becomes a strong advocate for Mother Earth and all her creatures. Fear and shame have no hold over her. She speaks her truth boldly, even in the face of criticism, and refuses to be silenced. This is the kind of female leader we need today.

Embodying the Mother

This morning, when you said, 'imagine the circle as a bowl of divine feminine energy,' I put myself in the bowl. I felt the divine mother there, and I was in the bowl, and I was asking her, "Can I really have healing? Can I?' And she was saying "Yes, yes, yes."

In our circles, we allow ourselves to be mothered, held, cherished, heard, seen and loved. Then, we extend that same love to others. Over and over we enact the ancient ritual of receiving and being received, containing and being contained, holding and being held, until we internalize the knowledge of love's abundant presence, and that inner knowing becomes so strong that we longer doubt or question it. After practicing Circlework for years, one woman told us:

The circle has given me an experience of love so deep, so complete. I've had experiences of nurturance and belonging before, but nothing like this. Before this, even when there was rain, there was always the fear of drought. Now my fear of drought is gone. That can't ever be taken away. I feel an entirely new dimension of love and trust. Something in me has been healed.

VOICES FROM THE CIRCLE

I used to be in the world in a very masculine way. I almost killed myself because I longed for the feminine but had no clue where to look so I became an alcoholic. But over the last twenty years, I've been finding a new way of doing things, of doing business, of hearing the voice of the feminine in me and in the world. It's very exciting. Now, I am a voice for the feminine.

We've spoken of the circle as an energetic amplifier that can intensify our perception of the sacred feminine and help us realize it as our own innermost nature. Occasionally, that presence becomes so strong that it catapults women into mystical states of union with the divine Mother. Their hands, voice and love then become the hands, voice and love of the goddess herself.

To witness this transformation of a human woman into her own essential divinity is one of the most moving experiences imaginable. In such moments, the artificial barriers that separate us from the realm of the deities melt and dissolve. As a woman realizes her own vastness she becomes a window through which other women, too, can realize their vastness. No mere human being, she becomes the embodiment of an ancient and universal cosmic force. Filled with awe, we then know ourselves to be in the presence of a great primordial mystery.

In the following transcript, you'll see this happening to a woman called Olga. Her journey begins when, guided by a dream, she decides to reach out to a former lover, a woman who has now come down with cancer.

We witness Olga as she cycles through three different ways of experiencing mother love. First, she expresses her desire to mother her former lover. At this point, she views herself as the giver, and her friend as the recipient.

Second, she embraces her own need for mothering. Now, the circle becomes the giver and she the recipient. From here, she moves into a state of spiritual ecstasy in which she transcends the duality of giving and receiving love to become a radiant embodiment of the Mother herself.

O: The night before last, I had a dream about my former lover Hannah, the woman I experienced such bliss with. After we broke up, she said she needed distance, so we haven't been in contact for a long time.

In my dream, we were looking for containers. There were teapots and other containers, and she was trying to find one that wasn't broken. I wasn't sure what those images meant but somehow, after that dream, I knew I had to call her. I wasn't sure she'd want to hear from me, but it felt important.

So yesterday, during our afternoon break, I called. It turned out she was very happy to hear from me. She told me that she'd had a complete hysterectomy a month ago and that they'd found a fast-growing type of ovarian cancer. She said she had just had her first chemotherapy treatment and was feeling nauseous. 'Last night was really hard,' she said.

I'm so glad I had the courage to call. This woman—I know every inch of her body. And that body that brought such ecstasy to both of us is now without a womb, and toxic chemicals are being poured into it. I can only imagine what she must be going through.

I want to ask her if she will just let me hold her and read her some of the poetry she loves. I hope she lets me. I want to hold her as a mother, not as a lover. I just want to infuse life force into her. I don't know if she will allow me to do that, but I would want it if I were in her place. More than anybody else, even more than my own mother, I would want her to come and hold me.

I'm afraid of being rejected, but I have to make my offering. If she doesn't want it that's okay. I trust whatever happens. It

VOICES FROM THE CIRCLE

For years, I avoided women's groups. I told myself I didn't like them, I wasn't the type and all this bullshit. It was a real shock when I realized that actually, I was running away from my feminine side. My mother always told me I wasn't beautiful. All my life, I pushed my femininity away and dismissed it as irrelevant. I focused only on my career and on my masculine energy. Now, I finally have the courage to stop and face myself. What would it mean to really own my feminine side? I so long to discover myself in a new way.

feels just as if one of my children were sick. Someone you love that much . . .

Olga is weeping. Then, she wipes away her tears and hands Jalaja the talking stone, indicating she's done.

J: (Gives the talking stone back to Olga.) Hold it a little longer, Olga. I'm so struck by the fact that you got this news now, here in the circle, right after you told us about that relationship and how much it meant to you. I understand your friend may be in need of mothering. But what about you? You too need mothering. She can't be a mother to you right now, but we can. Would you allow us to hold you in your grief?

Olga is weeping quietly. Jalaja holds her hand.

O: I'm not sure. I haven't thought about it. I've been so focused on supporting Hannah, you know. I haven't thought about myself.

J: Would you like to try letting us hold you and see how it feels?

O: Yes, I can try it. I guess I just don't know what to do.

J: You don't need to do anything. (To the other women): Let's make a space in the center for her.

The women lay down pillows and blankets. Olga lies down and immediately starts to sob.

J: (To the other women) Put your hands on her.

(To Olga) Let your sound out, let your sound out. Yes.

Olga wails. Everyone is holding and stroking her.

J: Let the sound come through, let all the sounds come through.

For a long time, Olga sobs and wails.

Then, she begins to speak.

O: (Gasping) I love you. I love you. Oh, my love . . . I see now that there's enough, there's enough, there's enough. There's enough love.

I thought there wasn't enough because my mother didn't give it to me. Now I understand that she loved me. All our mothers loved us, they just didn't know how. They tried. But I see now . . . I see . . . oh yes, I see. There's enough love for all of us. For all the babies, all the little ones. For all our bodies, for all our wombs. Oh, love, oh love, oh love . . .

For a minute or so, Olga sobs, too overcome to speak. Then she says:

I have never felt this before, this kind of love, this overwhelming, infinite love. This is how much we are loved. We need to know that. We need to know how very much we are loved. We need to let that love in, take it all in. How precious we are, how much our Mother wants us to know this. This is how much the Mother loves us, this is how much. This is how she feels for us when we suffer.

Someone wipes Olga's nose for her and says, "I'm just being the mother here." Laughter.

O: I want to see all you mothers. Please, hold me up, hold me up, I want to see us all.

The women help her sit up.

Oh yes, you're so beautiful. There are mothers everywhere. We're enough, we're enough, we're enough. Oh, all the babies, we love all the babies. Yes, yes, yes. Every day we need to make love with creation, every day, every day, every day. This is how big our love is. It's so healing, it's so healing. We are so loved, so infinitely loved, I never knew. Until now, I never, ever knew. Now I know. I know, Mother, and I will never forget your love ever again.

Feeling Safe

As a mother holds her baby, first in her womb and then in her arms, so the archetypal Mother is associated with the experience of feeling held, safe and secure.

From the perspective of our ego, there is no such thing as total safety. Death is, after all, an undeniable presence in our lives. And yet, we all know the subjective experience of safety. Perhaps we were lying on the forest floor on a warm summer evening and knew, in a way that had nothing to do with the rational mind, that everything was good and exactly as it should be. We knew that even if death were to appear, ready to claim us, that too would be completely safe—a simple, natural letting go into the arms of love.

With this awareness, I invite you to light a candle and invoke the presence of the sacred feminine in whatever way you are most comfortable with. Lie down, and become open to feeling a sense of complete safety and protection. Come home to the simplicity of your breath.

Imagine now that you are being held, in whatever way feels best to you. Invite your body and mind to relax into the embrace of love.

CHAPTER 6

Healing the Wounds of Rejection

When I'm frozen in terror, I find that I gain strength by acknowledg-
ing it out lout. If I can name it in the circle, then it starts to shift.

Few experiences cause such heartbreak as does rejection. It's bad
enough when we feel rejected by an individual we care about, be it a
parent, teacher, lover or friend. But when an entire community rejects
us, the pain can be devastating.

Thankfully, not everyone has experienced this particular brand of
suffering, but those who have never forget it. For me, it happened
when I was about seven years old. My family had just moved from
Vienna, Austria, to Santa Barbara, California, and though I spoke
English quite well, I still had a thick German accent. This, I soon discovered, was not a good thing.

The first day of school arrived. Then, the first recess. I stood shyly
on the playground, watching warily as a cluster of kids approached. A
fat boy with bright red hair began the interrogation. "What does your
father do? How many cars does he have?"

A girl with a long, sleek ponytail chimed in: "How many horses do
you have? I have three."

Anxiously, I shook my head. Just one beat-up old car. No horses.

"Not even one?"

No, not even one.

It took no time at all for my classmates to realize that I lacked all credentials for joining their club. I didn't have a rich family. I was shy and insecure.

And then, there was the accent. With World War II still fresh on people's minds, Germans weren't exactly popular. Soon, one of the boys started yelling: "Nazigirl! Nazigirl!"

I wasn't sure what that meant, but I knew it wasn't good. Only years later would I come to appreciate the irony that I, of all people, had been branded a Nazigirl. I was, in fact, the daughter of two Jewish parents, one of whom had fled the Nazis is 1938. But in that moment on the playground, all I knew was that I had been looked over and found wanting. Frightened and ashamed, I tried to hide my tears. My fate, however, was sealed. For the next year, I remained an untouchable and an outcast, target of hostility, ridicule and humiliation.

Such experiences are all too common; and many children are harshly rejected by their peers. Kristy, now in her eighties, still weeps at the memory:

> All these children surrounded me in a circle, and they all started poking me with their fingers, chanting the awful nickname they had come up with for me.

The cruelty of children is blunt, unsoftened by politeness and social niceties, and its effects can be devastating. Mariah tells us:

> I was a fat little girl, and I wore glasses. My self-confidence was pretty low to begin with, and somehow I always ended up being an outsider. I remember feeling so humiliated when teams got picked for games and neither side wanted me on their team. The teacher had to force them to take me."

Today, I am grateful for my own experience of group rejection, painful though it was, because it sensitized me to the issue. In my circles, I am quick to recognize the subtle signs that someone is feeling like an outsider.

Tribal Fear

Childhood trauma is one reason why we might be scared of groups, but it's not the only one. Sometimes, we might be sitting in circle when suddenly, for no apparent reason, we start to feel scared. We have no rational explanation for our feelings, and yet, they are undeniably real. Listen to Colleen, and you'll hear a woman in the grips of the kind of fear I'm talking about:

> I'm terrified of standing alone against a group and being scapegoated. I long to cling to the safety of the circle's acceptance. I'm constantly trying to control the process and structure it in such a way that people will approve of me and accept me. But the fear that they won't is enormous. I'm really scared. But why? I've never been scapegoated. Where is this coming from?

Where indeed? I believe the answer lies in the phenomenon I call *tribal fear*.

As we've discussed, the tribal era lasted far longer than any other stage in our evolutionary history. As a result, the lessons it taught us remain etched into our psyche, even to this day. During the tribal era, tribal rejection was more than just emotionally painful. Basically, it was a death sentence. Completely dependent on the support of our tribe as we were, being cast out was the ultimate calamity that could befall us.

And unfortunately, good behavior on our part didn't necessarily guarantee that we would be spared. Just like individuals, tribes can be highly enlightened and compassionate, but also heartless and cruel. At times, tribes may fall victim to a state of fear-fueled insanity that causes them to turn viciously on their own members. When that happens, the tribe becomes the worst enemy of those whom it has a mandate to protect and care for.

This tragic phenomenon has manifested thousands of times throughout human history. Even in modern times, we see the pattern repeating itself, be it in the murder of six million Jews in Germany or in the internment of thousands of Japanese Americans during WWII.

Today, tribal rejection remains a very real danger, especially in societies that retain a strong tribal flavor. My Indian dance teacher, who grew up in a tiny rural village in India, was terrified of it. She told me how easily a single woman might be condemned as a person of loose morals, and how such a loss of reputation would ruin her life. She would be treated with scorn when she came to buy her vegetables, and children would hurl insults at her as she walked down the street.

For untold millennia, we all learned the importance of staying in the good graces of our tribe and avoiding its rejection at all costs. Add to that the fact that most tribes gathered in circles, and you can appreciate why our feelings towards circles tend to be ambivalent. For millions of years, our tribal circle had the power of to protect and destroy us, to give life and take it. Is it any wonder that when we come to a circle, these old fears get activated?

Anyone who works with circles should be aware that they can trigger ancient wounds inflicted on our collective consciousness by experiences of tribal rejection. Yet in Circlework, we welcome the surfacing of tribal fear, because it means we're looking at an opportunity for healing one of the deepest collective wounds we carry. Of this healing process, we'll say more in a moment.

The Burning Times

I cannot speak of tribal fear without mentioning the so-called Burning Times, the period between 1550 and 1716, when thousands of women were condemned as witches and killed in the most gruesome ways. Anyone who works with women's circles or women's spirituality should be aware of the still festering wounds that were inflicted on our collective psyche during the Burning Times.

Some have claimed that up to six million women perished in the witch hunts. This appears be a gross exaggeration; modern scholars estimate that the death toll lies between 40,000 and 200,000. Yet these are still significant numbers, especially considering that back then, the total population of Europe was only around 90 million, and that for every woman condemned, thousands of others were haunted by the fear of meeting a similar fate.

The most trivial incident could provoke accusations of witchcraft, and suspects were often subjected to unspeakable torture. Maybe someone's child fell ill after having been touched by an aging spinster, or a man needed someone to blame his impotence on. The most vulnerable were single, elderly women who lacked protection, outsiders whom the community considered "strange," as well as midwives and healers.

Women, claimed the Church, were innately weak and sinful. Had not Eve eaten the forbidden fruit and thus become the instrument of Adam's downfall? Women were easy prey for Satan. The witch hunts sent them a clear message that anything short of complete obedience and submissiveness would not be tolerated. Any woman who demonstrated a sense of pride or appeared too powerful was a woman whose spirit needed to be broken.

What we lost, at this time, was not only a rich pre-Christian culture with its arts of herbalism and healing, midwifery and shamanism. Women also lost faith that their gifts would be appreciated and valued. In a terrifying reversal of justice, the most precious thing a woman could offer—her healing powers—became the cause of her death. Broken, also, was the solidarity of women, for in this atmosphere of terror and paranoia, women frequently delivered other women into the hands of the inquisition.

But the Burning Times didn't just stifle women's voices. A second, equally serious consequence was that they conditioned us to equate women's circles with witchcraft, an unfortunate association that lingers to this day.

Before the inquisition, women's circles were common, both

throughout Europe and around the world. Often, they followed the cycles of nature and were held in secluded natural settings. However, once the inquisition began, attending a women's circle became a dangerous and potentially life-threatening act.

In the eyes of the Church, ending women's ancient habit of gathering in circles was a crucial step towards holding them down and crushing their fiercely independent spirit. These circles, claimed church officials, were places of darkness and evil where women engaged in satanic rites. Therefore the mere accusation that a woman had gone to a circle gathering was enough to frame her as a witch.

So what exactly did women *really* do in their circles? Most men probably had only the foggiest notion. Still, for millennia, they honored women's ways because they saw that when the women returned, they were filled with goodness and light, and that these circles benefited the entire community. It is highly improbably that the unfortunate victims of the inquisition were engaged in Satanic rites. Most likely, women gathered, as had their foremothers, to sing and dance, heal and replenish. Presumably, they did many of the same things we do in our circles today—laugh, cry, celebrate and dance, until they felt empowered to go home and be the women they wanted to be.

But the Church did not want empowered women, nor did it like the innate egalitarianism of the circle. From its vantage point, the criminalization of women's circles was a tactically brilliant move. Cracking down on women's circles was one way to suppress remnants of the shamanic, nature-based spirituality that the indigenous European peoples had practiced long before the arrival of Christianity. At the same time, the witch hunts enforced submissiveness and deprived women of a tool for empowering themselves.

"Well," you might say. "At least today, we no longer burn witches at the stake."

Thankfully we don't, at least not in the West. Yet based on what I've experienced in my circles, I am convinced that many women remember the so-called burning times, as surely as Jews remember the

Jewish holocaust. Other female circle leaders have told me the same thing. Sherry Anderson, author of *The Feminine Face of God*, shared the following story from one of her circles:

> I led a retreat. Towards the end, one woman, an herbalist, told us that she felt she'd been holding back in our circle and had not had the courage to come forward with her gifts. I told her I sensed that lifetime after lifetime, she had brought her gifts forward, and they had been reviled. Nobody had wanted them, and people had mocked her. She started crying when I said this.
>
> Suddenly, I started seeing fires all around her. I was stunned. I didn't know what to say. Finally, I whispered: "I see these fires . . ." She just nodded. "I see them too," she said. And another woman agreed, "I see them too. They are witches fires, aren't they?"
>
> That was all we said. But throughout the rest of that day, I kept seeing those fires.

To accept such stories, we don't have to believe in past lives. We merely have to acknowledge that we don't fully understand exactly how memory is stored, and that somehow, our psyche *does* seem to remember events that we personally did not experience.

In my mind, there's no doubt that to a far greater degree than we usually realize, our psyche holds memories of events that occurred long before our own lifetime. The Burning Times, in particular, inflicted a major trauma on our collective psyche that still haunts us today. Unacknowledged, the fear we carry as its toxic residue can steal our voices, drive us into hiding, and keep us small.

The Burning Times were specifically intended to give women the message, once and for all, that submissiveness was their ticket to survival. So it's hardly surprising that today, when a woman stands on the threshold to empowerment, warning bells may go off in her psyche.

VOICES FROM THE CIRCLE

If someone rejects me, I think: yes, it's true, I'm a shitty person. If I weren't such a shitty person I wouldn't have done that and they wouldn't have rejected me. I abandon my inner child and I say: You did it again. You're really a bad girl and you need to stay in the corner until you shut up and do as you are told. If I can just be a good girl, everyone will like me.

But what the Burning Times taught us was not only to fear our feminine power, but also to fear circle gatherings. Indeed, it's one of the main reasons why many women, especially those steeped in Christian teachings, feel reluctant to engage in circle gatherings, even when doing so might immeasurably enrich their lives.

If you're interested in seeing more circles happen in your community, please bear in mind that the perception of those around you may well be tainted by conscious or unconscious fears. Learn to understand and address them, so that people can develop trust in the circle process. Often, all they need is a wee bit of reassurance: No, this is not a religious practice. No, this is not a cult. No, you will not be pressured to do anything you are uncomfortable with.

Overcoming Tribal Fear

Thankfully, we do have the wherewithal to heal the wounds of tribal rejection. However, I don't believe we can do it on our own—the wounds that were inflicted by in community must be healed in community. Whether we're scared of being burned at the stake, sent to a concentration camp or lynched and strung from a tree, this healing journey is one we can't take alone.

What are we to do when, suddenly, the old dragon of tribal fear rears its head and begins to pour its venom into our body and mind? The answer is simple: Tribal fear needs to be spoken. It needs to expressed and shared. If the circle can gently hold our fear in love, like a mother holds her frightened child, then it will most certainly begin to transform and dissolve.

In the Introduction, I told the story of how I spoke my fear in the presence of my therapy group, and how I finally was able to face the members of my circle, one by one, look them in the eye, and let them see me, with all my terror and grief.

Today, I wait for this moment of return in those I work with. This is the instant in which we shift from identifying ourselves as helpless victims to claiming our power—the power to face reality and respond with whatever intelligence, wisdom, and resourcefulness we possess. Instead of shrinking from the supposedly hostile gaze of others, we turn our own gaze towards them, allowing fear-based assumptions to be replaced by truthful perceptions. This choice to make eye contact is an important one because our willingness to see and be seen is the first step to connecting in intimate and authentic ways.

Often, our willingness to look people in the eye reflects our willingness to awaken from the nightmare of the past to the mystery of the present. Instead of projecting past experiences onto the present, we begin to open to the fresh, unpredictable gifts of the moment. Fearing the old, familiar pain of judgment or rejection, we lower our eyes. Once the windows of our soul are shuttered, we may feel a little safer, but the price we pay is blindness. If we looked, we might find acceptance and understanding. If we looked, we might discover that we have an inner strength capable of tolerating judgment and criticism. If we looked, we might realize the most painful judge is the one that lives within us.

Expressing tribal fear allows us to see clearly that though it can feel intensely personal, it is in fact not personal at all. Rather, our fear belongs to the circle, to the collective. Like any other wound it, too, must be washed in compassion, bathed in acceptance and offered into the light. One woman, after speaking her fear, tells us:

> I have let down my guard. Having expressed that I'm frightened has helped me be less so. Today I feel really relaxed and less self-conscious. My body feels better, and I'm more present. I feel good about being here.

What makes it possible for us to accomplish this healing journey today is that our circles are no longer tribal. Rather, they are what I

VOICES FROM THE CIRCLE

So much of my life I've waited for permission. Permission to speak, permission to wear this or that dress, permission to move ahead. . . . I always felt like I had to figure out how to make everybody else feel good, and then maybe, maybe I would have permission to do what I wanted. Now, I've stopped seeking permission from others. Circlework has given me permission to be me.

call third stage or planetary circles. Instead of being homogenous, like tribal circles, they may include people of various faiths, nationalities and belief systems.

VOICES FROM THE CIRCLE

It's hard for me to stand alone. This group feels safe enough for me to acknowledge this. I've had experiences of standing alone against the tribe, and being scapegoated.

Like our ancestors, we too depend on the support of a community. But today, our circles are not longer identical with our community, nor do they have the power of life or death over us that the tribal circle had. If some members of the circle don't like us, well, that's too bad, but it isn't the end of the world. We might feel terrified, but at least our rational mind understands that we're safe. Knowing that much less is at stake can give us the courage to be authentic, despite our fears.

Of course, a force as ancient and engrained as tribal fear will not vanish overnight. Many women experience tribal fear every time they come to a circle, and every time, they need to speak it, placing it into the bowl of the circle to be held and blessed. But though tribal fear may recur, we get better at recognizing it and seeing it for what it is. No longer cowed, we know that instead of hiding or running away, we can face it. Best of all, we know that every step we take towards its healing is a gift, not only to ourselves, but to the entire human family.

A Healing Ritual

Have you ever been wounded by tribal rejection—that is, rejection not just by an individual but by a group? If so, try performing the following ritual, or use these suggestions to create your own.

1 First, get a clear image of who you were when it happened. How old were you? What was your situation at the time?

2 Do you have an altar? If not, please create one for this practice. An altar is simply a focal point for your practice. Whether it's permanent or temporary, it should be clean and enjoyable to look at. Some people like to include lots of images, symbols and objects. Others prefer to keep it spacious, with just a candle or a flower. Creating altars is sacred play, so have fun with it and remember: You are going to use this altar as a place to acknowledge and honor the person who was wounded by tribal rejection. If you have any photographs of yourself from the time of your wounding, pull them up and place them on your altar.

3 When your altar is ready, get a glass of fresh water and sit down with your journal and pen at hand.

4 Begin by closing your eyes for a couple of minutes. Breathe deeply and hold the intention of offering healing energy to the person who was wounded, and to all people around the world who have been wounded in similar ways. Feel that this practice is an offering to them, too. As you consider your personal wounding, acknowledge the larger collective wound.

5 Once you feel centered and clear in your intention, imagine that you are holding in your heart the person you were when you were wounded. Notice her sorrow, her shame, her fear. Whatever feelings you find in her, simply acknowledge them and hold them in love. Breathe deeply, and make sure you are not just thinking about her but actually feeling her.

At the same time, remember that she is just one part of you: You are far more than just that wounded person. Feel your capacity to hold her, to be present with her, without drowning in her pain or merging with her. And know that to the extent that you can hold her, you can also hold all the other men, women and children who have been similarly wounded.

As you hold her in your heart, ask that she be healed, and that all be healed who feel that their community has rejected or betrayed them. Ask for healing on their behalf, as well as your own.

6 When you feel ready, open your eyes and pick up your writing materials. Now, invite the voice of love to speak through you and offer yourself as its scribe. Ask that voice to speak both to your former self and to all the rejected ones.

Don't rush or push. Just listen within, and wait to see whether any words want to rise up from deep within. If they do, write them down without censoring or editing. If they don't, that's fine too. There is no right or wrong way to do this practice. Just do what feels right to you.

Write for as long as you want. Then, place anything you wrote or drew on the altar. Feel: this is an offering of your personal truth to the source of healing. In a day or two, you may want to reread it.

7 Close by picking up the glass of water and holding in your hands. Take a moment to bless it and envision it as a healing potion and as liquid light. Ask that you, and all those who were wounded in similar ways, be completely healed. Affirm you yourself: May I be healed. May I be healthy. May I be whole in body, mind and spirit. End by drinking the water mindfully and with reverence for its healing powers.

CHAPTER 7

THE CIRCLE IN CHRISTIANITY

In my religious community, the congregation keeps getting smaller and smaller. Now it's dwindled to just a few senior citizens. The ministers are just pulling their hair over what to do about the lack of congregation. But it has never occurred to them to ask, "Where is the circle here?" There is no understanding of congregation as a co-creative field. The congregation is expected to be totally passive, so no power is generated.

Circlework is not a religious practice. Rather, it creates spaces where people of all faiths (or no faith) can share spiritual communion. The only prerequisite is that they must respect and honor all paths.

This, however, does not mean that Circlework can't be used in religious settings, or in conjunction with religious practices. The Circlework Training has attracted many religious leaders from diverse traditions who recognize the spiritual potency of the circle and want to share it with their communities. This pastor, for example, uses Circlework as the basis for the Interfaith circles she leads:

I think one of the most important gifts of Circlework is that it takes away all the argument about naming the Divine. Instead, you can just light a candle in the center, and then be together in that sacred presence. Circlework allows us to come together and acknowledge the significance of our relationship to Spirit, without needing to name it or subscribe to a doctrine. It gives people hope because it shows them they can have spiritual community, and they don't need to subscribe to a religious ideology to have it.

In a sense, using Circlework in religious settings is a no-brainer. There is, after all, no tradition that does not equate the circle with divinity. Just consider Islam, which forbids anthropomorphic images of God, but does allow the portrayal of God's beauty in the form of mandalas. Accordingly, Muslim artists have created some of the most breathtakingly gorgeous mandalas on our planet.

Today, at a time when millions of people feel spiritually famished, religious people of many faiths are experimenting with circle gatherings. In this chapter, I'm going to focus on Christian practice. However, a similar process of reclaiming the circle is occurring in all traditions.

Three Uses of Circle Gatherings in Spiritual Practice

◎ Circles can help religious groups rediscover and deepen their spirituality.

◎ Circles can help non-religious people build spiritual community.

◎ Circles allow members of diverse persuasions to come together in sacred space.

John's Circle

Christianity has a long history of revering the circle and honoring its spiritual potency. The beautiful stained glass windows of medieval cathedrals, for example, were not conceived as mere ornaments, but rather as visual songs of praise for a God whom theologians defined as "the circle whose center is everywhere and circumference nowhere." In fact, the awareness of the circle as a tool for facilitating sacred remembrance is built into our very language. Consider, for example, the word "meditation," which is derived from the Latin *meditare*, which means "going to the center."

The awareness of the circle as a sacred image is firmly rooted in Christian tradition. Yet as we discussed in the last chapter, Christians also bear the burden of the fact that for several centuries, the Church waged a veritable war on circles. Naturally, this has had a profound impact on Christian practice. Mention circle gatherings, and many Christians will recoil, as if it they'd been asked to participate in a Satanic rite. And in recent decades, the Church has once again been cracking down hard on Catholic nuns who choose to celebrate mass in the round.

And yet, the fact is that circle gatherings have a long-standing role in Christian worship. By gathering in a circle, Christians are simply returning to the roots of their tradition. For example, according to the Acts of John, a text originally included in the New Testament but later rejected by the Church as heresy, Jesus himself led circle gatherings for his disciples.

It happened, John claims, shortly before Jesus was crucified. Gathering his disciples around him, Jesus asked them to form a circle and to dance around him while he stood in the center.

The center of a circle symbolizes the Source, the One, the Divine. So by standing in the center, Jesus was affirming his identity with the Divine and with the eternal, deathless source. He did this, not for himself alone, but on behalf of all beings. "What I am, you too are," he told his followers. "Remember this, and do not get swept up in the drama that is about to unfold."

This, at least, is how I understand the meaning of this extraordinary text. But such a potent piece of scripture is worth quoting first hand:

VOICES FROM THE CIRCLE

Jesus told us to love our enemies. But I don't believe anyone can love their enemy as long as they see them only as that: an enemy. To love our enemy, we must first recognize them as human beings. We must understand that no matter how much we might disagree, we have a lot in common. We need circles, because this knowledge cannot be acquired from a distance. We have to sit face to face with our enemies, hear their story, and understand their motivations.

Before Jesus was arrested . . . he assembled us all, and said, "Before I am delivered to them, let us sing a hymn to the Father, and so go to meet what lies before us." So he told us to form a circle, holding one another's hands, and he himself stood in the middle and said, "Answer Amen to me." So he began to sing the hymn and to say,

VOICES FROM THE CIRCLE

I'm a Rabbi. In my professional role, I can't really share my fears and my grief. For me, the circle provides an opportunity to let my tears out, to voice my fear, to be held, to be sung to. I needed a community where it was safe to explore my own spirituality, and to witness others exploring theirs, without being the leader. That is so important to me.

Glory be to thee, Father.
And we circled around him, and answered him, Amen.

Glory be to thee, Logos:
Glory be to thee, Grace. Amen.

Glory be to thee, Spirit:
Glory be to thee, Holy One:
Glory be to thy Glory. Amen.

We praise thee, Father:
We thank thee, Light:
In whom darkness dwelleth not. Amen.

And why we give thanks, I will tell you.
I will be saved,
And I will save. Amen.
I will be released,
And I will release. Amen.
I will be wounded,
And I will wound. Amen.
I will be born,
And I will bear. Amen.
I will eat,
And I will be eaten. Amen.

I will pipe,
Dance, all of you. Amen.

I will mourn,
Beat you all your breasts. Amen.

The twelfth number
dances on high. Amen.

To the universe
belongs the dancer. Amen.

Whoever does not dance
does not know what happens. Amen.

I am a mirror to you
who know me. Amen.
I am a door to you
who knock on me. Amen.
I am a way to you,
the traveler. Amen

Now if you follow my dance,
see yourself
in Me who am speaking,
and when you have seen what I do,
keep silence about my mysteries . . .

You who dance, consider
what I do, for yours is
this passion of humanity
which I am to suffer.

For you could by no means
have understood what you suffer
unless to you, as the Word,
I was sent by the Father . . .
What I am you shall see
when you come yourself.

So then I have suffered none of those things which they will say of me; even that suffering which I showed to you and to the rest in my dance, I will that it be called a mystery.[1]

A Modern-Day John

As we have seen, the Church did its best to suppress circle gatherings and to impose hierarchical religious structures. Today, most Christian churches have built-in pews to ensure that instead of connecting with each other, people will face the robed figure up front. And as we mentioned, many Christians are afraid of circles and of what they evoke. Debra, a pastor and circle leader, says:

> The biggest challenge in my church is that people are terribly afraid of intimacy with each other and Spirit. God knows I've been scared of it myself so I can appreciate their fear. As I see it, a lot of traditional religion is geared towards actually preventing that intimacy, that direct encounter with something that is uncontrollable, unpredictable, and sometimes terrifying. It takes a lot of sensitivity and skill to introduce this work to people without scaring them.

Still, a hunger as raw and essential as the need for communion with the sacred cannot be denied forever, and today, many Christians are beginning to courageously reclaim their heritage. Another pastor says:

> In my ministry, I now do all of my small group work in circles. I'm also moving towards bringing circle dances to our contemporary worship service. I try to provide multiple opportunities for people in Christian community to sit in circle with one another. I believe Circlework can allow people to open up to difference, and to find it a beneficial experience, as opposed to a threatening experience.

John, too, is a pastor who regularly facilitates circle gatherings for his congregation. "People need a safe place where they can explore their spirituality," he says. "They need a place where they don't just talk but really share from the heart. A place where tears are welcome and where they don't have to put up a façade."

When I ask John where his love of circles comes from, he tells me about a powerful spiritual awakening he experienced as a young college student.

I grew up in a normal middle-class Protestant church. Every week I would go to church. It had no special meaning to me, but it felt like a good thing to do. Just after WW II, I also joined the local youth group at church. I wasn't really spiritual though. I joined mainly because it was a great place to meet girls.

Some of the men from this church group were planning to go on a retreat together. I thought this sounded nice, so I decided to join them. We went by ourselves, a bunch of guys without a leader. We spent two and a half days at a center in Pennsylvania. I had never done anything like this before, and the whole thing was completely foreign to me. Most of our time was spent in silence, and this too was a new experience for me. We would sit in a circle around these big tables to talk or meditate.

Near the end of the time we celebrated communion. Some of the guys just did this, without the help of any clergy. Of course I had experienced communion in church many times. But never before had I done it in a circle, and it had never meant much to me before.

But now, it suddenly it struck me that here we were, just as Jesus must have been around the table with his friends. He was telling them that he was going to die, and what the meaning of communion was.

VOICES FROM THE CIRCLE

I have left my church. You know, it was always about trying to be good and avoiding judgment. When I discovered Circlework, I was so moved by the way we see each person as a unique, human self, but also as a manifestation of the Divine. Relating to people in both ways at once is an amazing experience. Now, I am beginning to perceive people in general that way. That is something I never experienced in my religious community.

As we were drinking the wine and breaking the bread I was overwhelmed with emotion. I thought, "I am taking this man into myself, I am making him part of me. And I am part of a circle of people who are doing this in community, and this is what communion is really all about."

My God, this was a brand new awareness for me, and it moved me so deeply! It initiated an understanding that would never have arisen in a church setting where people sit in rows.

This happened over fifty years ago. Today, I sit every morning with a picture of Jesus that I love very much. It's a Rembrandt, and it shows Jesus sitting at a table, holding communion with two disciples after his resurrection. He is looking straight at you with these very powerful eyes.

This picture takes me right back to that experience of sharing communion in circle. Again, I feel I am sitting around the table with Jesus, and I become part of his circle, and I receive into myself the essence of resurrection, the essence of death that has been transmuted into life.

Listening to John, I think of his namesake, John the Disciple, who two thousand years earlier gathered in a circle around his soon-to-die teacher. That circle still echoes through the hearts and souls of people like John the pastor, who feels Christ's presence and blessing whenever he sits in circle within his community. Like millions of religious people around the world, he considers the circle a friend and ally, a guide to wholeness and a portal into sacred space.

CHAPTER 8

RECLAIMING OUR VOICE

It's invaluable to have a place where I can speak honestly and be heard and received. It is helping me be more courageous out here, in the world. I am taking more risks, speaking out more. I am seeing our work in the circle transfer to the rest of my life.

We've spoken of the six geometric elements that comprise our mandala in Circlework. Each one is a powerful teacher in its own right, with its own messages and gifts. But among them, the Heaven-Earth axis plays a key role—especially for women, and especially at this time in history.

In a nutshell, the Heaven-Earth axis is the channel of energy and life force that runs vertically through the center of your body. If you were a tree, it would be your trunk. Moving downward, it anchors you in the earth. Moving upward, it connects you with the heavens.

Your voice, in turn, is the audible manifestation of your Heaven-Earth axis. When your Heaven-Earth axis is strong, your voice will sound full and resonant. Vice versa, any blockages within your Heaven-Earth axis will directly impact your voice.

You may never have heard of the "Heaven-Earth axis" before. But you're surely familiar with the concept, because it's embedded in our speech. For example, when we describe someone as "upright" or "upstanding," or as "having a strong backbone," we're not referring to their physical body, but to the strength of their Heaven-Earth axis.

VOICES FROM THE CIRCLE

I'm a singer. But in the circle, I learned more about singing than in any class I ever took because here, I found my true voice.

Similarly, when we say that someone "has no voice in the matter," we're not implying that they can't speak, but that they're powerless.

What is the Heaven-Earth Axis?

◎ Physically, the Heaven-Earth axis is the vertical line that runs through the center of your body, through your head, spinal column and legs.

◎ Energetically, the Heaven-Earth axis reflects your personal power and vitality.

◎ Emotionally, the Heaven-Earth axis manifests as authenticity, integrity, confidence and courage.

◎ Individually, the Heaven-Earth axis reflects your uniqueness and your existential aloneness. A strong Heaven-Earth axis empowers you to show up, speak out and stand up for what you believe in—if need be, alone.

◎ Spiritually, the Heaven-Earth axis represents your personal connection to the universe, God, Spirit and the Self.

Today, our world urgently needs women to stand up and speak out. This, however, they can only do if their Heaven-Earth axis is strong. When a woman's Heaven-Earth axis is strong, so is her voice. She's not afraid to share her truth, nor does she doubt her right to exist, to take up space, to have an opinion and to voice it. She knows that sharing her truth is an important aspect of why she has incarnated, and she's committed to showing up fully and authentically. She recognizes her weaknesses and flaws, but she also knows her worth and is not ashamed of who she is.

People with a strong Heaven-Earth axis possess integrity, confidence and courage. Their force field is charged with vitality, and when they speak, others take notice. They can tolerate conflict, will stand up for what they believe in, and care more about self-respect than outer accolades. Such people make bad subjects for totalitarian dictators. Unafraid of speaking their minds, they are not easily manipulated or silenced by outer authorities. Within their communities, they are the guardians of integrity. No democracy can survive without them, and in the long run, no dictatorship can withstand them.

All the great beings who changed our world for the better, from Jesus to Martin Luther King, had a rock-solid Heaven-Earth axis. Consider Mahatma Gandhi, who in 1906 vowed that he would henceforth defy unjust and discriminatory laws imposed by the British, even if it cost him his freedom or his life. Though thousands took the same vow with him, he swore that if need be, he would defend his convictions by himself. "I believe," he said, "that standing up for the truth is the greatest thing in the world." These are the words of a man who stood unwavering in his Heaven-Earth axis.

Traditionally, the Heaven-Earth axis has been associated with the masculine principle. It's the erect phallus, the pillar of mystical light, the power of pure presence, the Shivalingam. In contrast, the receptive circumference is traditionally associated with the feminine, and with symbols such as the protective womb and the nurturing breast.

Within the mandala of our communities, women have long been the keepers of the circumference. This was their designated role: they were the peacekeepers, the ones who made sure everyone got along and who kept the family together. Protecting the circumference of our families and communities is, without doubt, a sacred task. However, so is embodying the Heaven-Earth axis by standing up, speaking out, and making our unique contribution to the world, whatever it might be.

Ideally, no one should have to pick one over the other. There is no reason we can't pursue our personal dreams, ambitions and goals while also serving the well-being of our families and

Voices from the Circle

As a child, I stuttered badly, and until recently, I could never introduce myself without stuttering. Today, I understand that I lost my voice when I lost my power. When I say my name, it's like I'm announcing my presence. I'm saying: Here I am, look at me! I'm claiming space for myself. In my family, that was never okay. A year ago, when our circle met for the first time, I burst into tears when I had to say my name. Until I came here, I never knew what unconditional support felt like. In the circle, I can now say my name easily. I can be me, and I can let you see me as I am. And slowly, I'm starting to trust that I can show up elsewhere, too. My confidence has grown immensely. I can walk in with pride and say: I am Paula. This is who I am.

communities. In order to love others, we don't need to abandon ourselves. Yet sadly, this is precisely what many of our mothers and grandmothers were forced to do, and what is even today expected of women in many parts of the world.

VOICES FROM THE CIRCLE

It's been so powerful to reclaim my voice. Not only can I sing, but I don't feel ashamed. That's what's different. I don't feel ashamed of my voice. That intense old grief that came out of me—I could never make that sound before, or anything close, except during sex. Freeing my voice has opened up a whole other range of being for me.

However, change is in the air. I believe that the collective intelligence of our species recognizes how important it is that women's voices be heard. And so, women everywhere are beginning to show up in ways they never did before.

In the past, patriarchy has often judged women harshly for daring to claim powers supposedly reserved for men. Thankfully, those old stereotypes are now beginning to dissolve. Still, many women who come to my circles aren't sure they have the right to stand strong in their Heaven-Earth axis. In theory, they might believe it—but in practice, they're hesitant. Maybe they were taught that rage is not "feminine." Maybe they were chastised for being too passionate or assertive. A woman, they learned, is supposed to be soft-spoken and sweet, alluring to men and good with children.

In the following transcript from the Circlework Training, I talk about this issue. "To have power," I say, "We must have a voice."

Of course we all *do* have a voice. But is it our true voice? Many of us have lost touch with our true voice. We learned that others didn't want to hear it, so we created a watered-down, weakened, censored, diminished version that we believed would be more acceptable.

When you're speaking with your true voice, you can feel the vibration throughout your entire body, not just in your throat and chest but also your belly. Your true voice rises up from the earth like a fountain, clear and resonant. When you speak with your true voice, people pay attention. Even if you speak softly, your true voice will convey a sense of authority. Whether or not others agree is beside the point. When you're speaking in your true voice, they'll listen. That voice isn't always nice or sweet or pretty, but it's authentically yours.

In this chapter, I'd like to introduce you to a number of women who, thanks to their women's circles, found their voice in a new way. For a variety of reasons, they had all lost their authentic voice. But in each case, the listening and encouragement they received from their circle was the key ingredient that allowed them to leave muteness and obscurity behind.

Annette and Geneen

What does an empowered woman actually look like? How do we embody our power bravely and boldly? We can easily point to examples of powerful women who emulated men's ways, acting and talking like men. It's much harder to find role models of women who remained true to their feminine nature and embodied the sacred feminine in the world.

One evening, during a Circlework Training, I asked whether anyone knew of a woman who fully embodied her Heaven-Earth axis, and who wasn't afraid to stand up and use her voice. "If you know someone like that," I suggested, "tell us a story about them."

I looked around at the women's faces, softly illumined by candle light—faces that a few days ago were those of strangers, yet now seemed achingly dear. There was a long moment of silence. Then, Annette spoke up.

"I have a story," she said. As we settled into our seats, she began:

It's a story about my mother. She is no longer alive, she died seven years ago. My mother was this tiny 100-pound woman, but she could have been the commander of an army, honest and truly, that was her nature. Boy, could she ever be fierce!

So one day we're walking through town, meaning downtown New York. I must have been about ten years old at the time. So there's this subway station, and right there, at the top of the stairs, is this big black man, and he's yelling at his girlfriend. I'd say he looked to be about sixteen. He had a lit cigarette that he was holding up to her face and he was threatening to burn her with it. See, this was in the middle of New York City, so people were just walking by and letting this happen. They were totally ignoring what was going on, because that's what it's like. People are afraid of getting involved.

But my mother didn't think twice. She just marched up to this guy and grabbed the cigarette out of his hand. Then, she stuck it under his own chin and she yelled, "How does that feel, eh?"

This guy was so taken aback by this little white woman pouncing on him like that, that he just froze. But that wasn't all. Then she started scolding him, as if he were a little child. She was yelling at him, "Don't ever do that to anyone ever again, do you hear me? Never again!"

All the while she's just glaring at him and she's holding him against the wall with the burning cigarette under his chin. That was my mother. My mother could do things like that, she had that kind of courage. There was nobody she wouldn't stand up to.

As Annette tells her story, I notice that Geneen is quietly weeping. A young African-American woman raised in an extremely abusive family, Geneen learned at an early age that invisibility was her ticket to safety. Now, she's gradually beginning to find her voice. Still, she's terrified of being the center of attention. Unless someone puts her on the spot, she tends to remain silent. But Annette's story has opened something up in her.

"You probably all identify with Annette's mom," she says.

But I'm right there with the girlfriend. I know what it's like to have no voice and to feel like if I say anything, I'm gonna get killed.

Being in this circle with you all has been so amazing. Sometimes I'm so emotional I have no words. In those moments,

I don't even know how to tell you that I'm feeling emotional. But you have been really good at asking: "Where are you, Geneen?" Your asking makes it possible for me to admit: "I'm an emotional wreck right now." Can I allow myself to say that? To actually speak the truth out loud? I am learning that I can, and that you won't reject me when I do.

Joanne

Looking at Joanne, you would probably think: "That woman has a strong Heaven-Earth axis." Her voice sounds confident and she has no problem talking about just about anything.

However, for many years, the doors to certain chambers within her psyche always remained locked. Joanne is by no means alone. Out of shame, many women cordon off certain parts of their lives. They believe that if someone were to discover certain truths about them, they would surely be rejected.

Of course, we have every right to be discerning about what we share with others. But it's a sad, lonely state of affairs when we hide certain issues, even from our closest sisters—not because they aren't important, but because we're too ashamed to speak. Fortunately, over time, a level of trust can develop in a women's circle that causes those inner prison walls to crumble. So it was for Joanne:

The deepest, darkest, worst, most shameful, most horrendous secret of my life was, without doubt, my husband's physical abusiveness. I was way too ashamed to share this with my friends and community. I felt so ashamed of myself, as well as protective of him.

For a long time, I never mentioned the abuse in our circle, either. But at some point, someone asked me about it, and I told the truth. That was a real turning point. Oh, it was such a relief!

VOICES FROM THE CIRCLE

I've been going for job interviews. When I focus on who I think I'm supposed to be in order to qualify for these jobs, I get stuck. I feel afraid and my voice gets weak. But if I can get grounded and stay connected to my Heaven-Earth axis, something shifts. Then I no longer feel like a child who is being judged. I feel confident and I can speak up for myself.

I had felt so lonely. Now I didn't feel lonely anymore. The women came to me and supported me in a way that I had never known was possible.

Sharing my secret also made me feel much, much safer because I knew that if my husband ever became abusive again, I could call on my sisters for help and I would have a safe haven.

It also changed my husband's behavior. When I came home from that circle, he intuitively knew that I had gained a whole new level of strength. I was stronger within myself, but also, the women in the circle now represented a refuge for me, a place I could go to if I ever needed to. And this meant I would no longer be in a state of complete dependency.

Meera

Meera was raised in Pakistan, in a very conservative, traditional family where women were supposed to be beautiful yet mute. Though she was never beaten or physically abused, she was given to understand, in no uncertain terms, that her voice was unwelcome. As a child, she was never allowed to shout or yell, and even as an adult, her voice was soft and weak.

Meera had arrived in the United States a few years ago with her American husband. Bright and well educated, she soon secured a good job at a bank. Yet she dreamed of doing something very different. "I want to work for the earth," she said. "I want to work for the environment."

How, I wondered, would this young woman ever speak up in defense of the planet? Right now, she could barely speak up for herself. In the circle, we kept asking her to raise her voice because we couldn't hear her.

Meera told us that at work, she tried to act strong, but that actually, she still felt like a shy little girl. As she watched our interactions, she marveled at the apparent ease with which American women spoke their minds and expressed their wants and needs. For her, this was a huge challenge—especially in relationship to men. "I have a problem with men," she told us:

> In my culture, men don't do anything in the household. When my father takes a bath, he just leaves everything on the floor and we women are supposed to clean up after him. When he comes to visit me in the States, he expects me to be a full time servant in the household, even though I have a job.

Meera didn't like being treated as a servant. And yet, she didn't really feel she had the right to say no. For too long, she'd been expected to serve the men in her household. Yet in our circle, she found a haven where she could practice speaking her truth in a safe supportive environment—not just once, but over and over. Often, she was overwhelmed by doubt: Did she really have the right to share her thoughts and feelings? Was it really okay to show up authentically?

At every meeting, we kept encouraging her to voice whatever was on her mind, without worrying what might come out of her mouth. Over the months, we learned about her upbringing, her family, and her struggle to speak honestly with her father. To us, it was all fascinating, and we listened with rapt attention. As Meera realized that we sincerely appreciated her, and wanted to hear from her, she began to develop a new sense of confidence. Gradually, she started to trust that her voice really *did* matter, and was just as important and valuable as anyone else's.

Her growing strength was evident. However, her father was far away, in Pakistan. What, I wondered, would happen when he decided to come for a visit?

I needn't have worried. One day, Meera reported, glowing with pride, that her dad had been in town and that, for the first time in her life, she had stood up to him. "I was gentle and polite," she assured us. "But I was clear."

VOICES FROM THE CIRCLE

I don't know whether you heard me screaming in the woods. Anne and I went out for a walk last afternoon. We're way out there and suddenly Anne says, "Oh, did you know there are wolves out here?" (*Laughter*) I just started screaming at the top of my lungs. "Hush," she said, "somebody's going to hear!" And I said, "That's the whole point!" It was wonderful to be able to do that. I am very, very grateful for all of you for helping me reclaim my voice.

As you all know, on my father's previous visits, I always went along with his expectations. But last month, when he announced he'd be returning for another visit, I decided that this time, I would speak up about the things that bothered me. For example, I wanted to tell him that it was important to me that he clean up after himself in the bathroom.

For me to speak to my father about this was huge. To you, it probably sounds like a very small thing, but to me, it was a really big deal. My father is hot-headed and when he flies into a rage he can be terrifying. The instant he raises his voice I choke up and cannot speak at all. I completely lose my voice and turn into a little girl.

So when I decided to speak to him about the bathroom issue, everything in me was screaming, "Are you crazy? Have you lost your mind?" And I could hear the voice of my relatives, "How can you say this to your father? America is spoiling you. Come on, just clean up after him."

But I didn't want to. It didn't feel right. I never had a voice before. But now, I'm no longer willing to stay silent. I imagined all of you with me, and it gave me so much courage.

My father didn't say much but he listened without flying off the handle. Once I had said what I needed to say, I didn't care whether he agreed or not. Just being able to speak made me feel so powerful. It's still hard for me to speak up, instead of swallowing my feelings, but I'm learning, and I'm proud of myself.

To witness Meera's evolution was like watching patriarchy crumble before our very eyes. On the one hand, the circle gave Meera a place to speak. But equally importantly, she needed to be heard. How powerful is the simple act of supportive, attentive listening! When we are heard in this way, we begin to speak from a deeper place of greater authenticity. This is why the experience of being deeply heard, not just once but repeatedly, can give us the strength and confidence we need to show up in the world.

Jessie

Like Meera, Jessie, too, grew up in an environment that stifled her voice. In Jessie's case however, rigid patriarchal values weren't to blame. The problem was simply that Jessie's family was large, loud and rambunctious. In this environment, quiet people like Jessie didn't stand a chance. "When I was growing up, I could never get a word in edgewise," she recalls. And so, she clammed up.

"Because I wasn't being heard, I eventually stopped trying to express myself. My reaction to not being heard was to either not talk at all, or to talk in a way that said, 'I know you're going to tune me out any second now.'"

But when Jessie joined our circle, she, like Meera, discovered that other women actually *wanted* her to claim her authentic voice.

One day, while I was talking in the circle, I realized: "They're all listening to me!" This seems obvious, but it felt huge. In a way it was paralyzing and overwhelming. At the same time it was also enormously healing. It was the first time I'd ever experienced deep listening. When I saw that in the circle, people were truly paying attention and waiting to hear what I had to say, I thought, "Oh, I guess I'd better take myself seriously, too."

I began practicing the idea that in the circle, people might actually want to hear me. I started acting as though they did, instead of assuming that they didn't. At the same time, the circle helped me listen more deeply into myself so that I could hear what I really wanted to say.

After practicing in the circle, I gradually became able to speak that way outside of the circle, too. Instead of expecting others to lose interest, I learned to wait until I had something to say, and then say it with the conviction that it had value. This is huge for me because it's allowed me to claim my voice in the world. I've become much more outspoken in my church, and in the world in general, about who I am and what I'm doing and what my values are. I'm not afraid of showing up.

Every time I see a woman finding her voice in the circle, I rejoice, not only for her sake but for all of us. At this time in history, women's voices need to be heard. We need to speak out on behalf of the earth and on behalf of future generations. But for this to happen, we need support.

We're amazed when we witness the courage of a girl like Malala from Pakistan, who stood up to the Taliban and refused to be silenced. But let's not forget that Malala was raised by a father who gave her unconditional love and supported her every step of the way.

Today, there are millions of potential Malalas. Most of them didn't receive the kind of parenting that allowed Malala to become a powerful voice for women's rights. But fortunately, we don't have to depend only on our parents for this kind of empowerment. With the support of a caring circle, millions of women could reclaim their voice and their power. Our world would be a better place for it—of that, I have no doubt.

Showing Up

Before we can show up authentically, we need to become conscious of how we hide. Nothing wrong with hiding—sometimes, it's a smart thing to do. The question is: Are we hiding consciously? Is it our choice? Or are we caught up in old habits that may no longer serve us?

Today, pay close attention to when you hide, how you hide and what it feels like. Every time you notice you are hiding, give yourself a blessing. Say to yourself:

"Dear one, I see that in this moment, you are hiding. I promise to love and accept you fully, no matter what. If you chose to stay in hiding, I shall bless your choice. But I will bless you equally if you decide to take a step towards greater visibility. No matter how the world responds, I will be here to support you. I will applaud your courage and celebrate your magnificence."

CHAPTER 9

MIRRORING THE LIGHT

If we knew how to adore, then nothing could truly disturb our peace. We would travel through the world with the tranquility of the great Rivers.

St. Francis of Assisi

In my circles, I often tell myths about goddesses from around the world. Among them, one of my favorites is the story of the Japanese sun goddess Amaterasu. Not only is it extremely relevant for any woman who finds herself on a healing journey, but it's also a beautiful allegory of what Circlework is all about.

Amaterasu the sun goddess was greatly beloved by the Japanese people, especially by the rice farmers who would set up altars for her amidst their fields, where they offered prayers for a good harvest.

Amaterasu, so the story goes, had a brother, Susanowo, who bitterly resented his sister's popularity. To make matters worse, he was a mean alcoholic. One night, he went out drinking, and the more he drank, the more his jealousy swelled like a balloon. Finally, puffed up with a sense of righteous rage, he set out on a rampage that left Amaterasu's temples across the land in ruins, covered in mud and shit.

It wasn't the first time this had happened. Yet for Amaterasu it was

VOICES FROM THE CIRCLE

I will always carry with me the incredible variety and beauty of these women, each one so unique and amazing. At first, I was able to see the soul quality, the essence, in only one or two. Now I see it in everyone. I perceive their light, and if I close my eyes, I can see their colors.

the straw that broke the camel's back. Her mood turned black and she sunk into a deep depression.

"I've had it," she announced. "I'm out of here."

Then, she strode off and climbed up high into the mountains. There, she sought out a cave. After entering it, she sealed off the entrance with a huge boulder. Instantly, the world was plunged into darkness and icy cold. People shivered in the rice fields as their terrified children clung to them.

At first, nobody knew what to do. But eventually, word got out about what had happened and where Amaterasu had sought refuge.

"Let's go," the people said. Wrapping themselves in their warmest clothes, they set out for the high mountains.

Soon, thousands had congregated in front of Amaterasu's cave. Stomping their feet to keep warm, they started singing her praises. Maybe, they thought, they could appease her and make her change her mind. The musicians piped up, and before you knew it, everyone was doing the ancient whirling dances that mimic the course of planets as they circle the sun.

"Please, Amaterasu, come out," they cried over and over. "Please, don't abandon us. We love you!"

But Amaterasu didn't respond. Despondent, she sat in her cave, too sad to care what was going on outside.

Hours passed. Someone brought a keg of beer. The party—for that was what it had become—turned ever more wild and raucous. In any case, it was far too cold and dark for people to work. So young and old decided to celebrate their goddess.

Well. As everyone knows, Amaterasu the sun goddess loves a good party. And as time went on, she started feeling a little bored, sitting there all by herself in her cave. A tiny spark of curiosity rose up in her.

"What's going on out there?" At first, she just shrugged.

"I don't care," she said.

But after a while, she decided she would take a quick peek and

Voices from the Circle

It makes me sad to realize how I've been missing out on people. I mean, if I'd seen you on the street or in some other context I would just have passed you by and would not have been interested. I would never have seen all the wisdom and caring and love that is here.

check out the scene. "Nobody will notice," she thought.

Now obviously, this is absurd. How could one not notice the appearance of the sun in the dark of night?

But like so many of us, Amaterasu didn't really know the brilliance and magnificence of her own light. So, she stood up, walked to the entrance, and cautiously rolled the boulder aside, just enough so she could peek out.

This was the moment the people had been eagerly awaiting! With them, they had brought a huge octagonal mirror. The second they saw Amaterasu's rays shooting out of the cave like golden arrows, they immediately hoisted the mirror high into the air. And so, Amaterasu's light came bouncing back into her own eyes.

At first, the goddess had no idea what she was looking at. Stunned by the radiance and beauty of this golden light, and wanting to take a closer look, she took a step out of her cave. Instantly, the brilliance of the light increased. Another step, and another.

And slowly, it began to dawn on Amaterasu that she herself might be the source of this golden glory.

"That light . . ." she asked, her voice filled with wonder. "Is that . . . Is that me?"

"Yes!" the people cried. "Yes, glory be to you, goddess, this is your light!"

Thus Amaterasu came to realize her true beauty and magnificence. Filled with the knowledge of her own light, her depression lifted and she became happy once again. And so, the people were able to escort their beloved goddess back to her heavenly home. To this very day, Amaterasu's mirror is one of the three sacred treasures that the Japanese emperor holds in his safekeeping.

We all know what it feels like to be treated with disrespect. Like Amaterasu, we too have been hurt and insulted. People have broken our hearts or destroyed things we held precious. We too have been pelted with shit.

The soul is resilient, yes. But when we are put down again and again, our soul gets depressed and withdraws. Outwardly, we might seem fine. Yet our inner world feels bleak, dark, and cold.

Countless people live in this state. Without the healing mirror that might reveal their light, their soul remains mired in grief. Like Amaterasu, it is sitting in a dark cave, alone and in despair.

Psychologists have long emphasized the fact that children need positive mirroring. But adults need it too. We too need to see the reflection of our own light in the eyes of others, to feel seen and appreciated. Otherwise, our soul becomes engulfed in darkness and depression.

I call this process sacred mirroring or "seeing with sacred eyes." In sacred mirroring, we're not looking at a person's ego, but rather at their deepest essence. You might also say that we're looking *through* them, all the way to the place where we're one. What divine qualities do we see in them? Joy? Courage? Wisdom? Whatever we find, as we look at them, belongs to us, as well. For just as beauty lies in the eye of the beholder, so do all sacred qualities: The light we see in others is our own.

But to merely glimpse another's inner radiance is not enough. We must also give words to what we see. We all carry the seeds of divine qualities within us, but in order to sprout and grow, they need to be acknowledged and appreciated. By naming and celebrating a woman's inner light, we help her embrace it.

Circlework helps us realize, in profound and sometimes life-changing ways, how beautiful we really are and how amazing our light is. All beings are beautiful, of course. But women possess a special kind of magic. Women are innately mysterious and miraculous. The circle opens our eyes to this truth, and prepares us to view women outside of the circle with new eyes, as well.

You might imagine that this affirmation of our magnificence would lead to ego-inflation and arrogance. Yet actually, the opposite is true. Reverence for the soul allows for a very liberating kind of irreverence towards the personality. When we feel seen and loved, our need to protect and defend the dark corners and shadows of our ego diminishes drastically.

At some point, we all encountered someone who saw and validated our basic goodness: a teacher who acknowledged our potential, a lover who saw our inner beauty, an acquaintance who pointed out something special in us that no one else had ever noticed. I'm not talking about flattery, here. The flatterer tells us what we would like to believe is true, but may not be. In contrast, sacred mirroring reminds us of important truths we need to remember. To be seen in this way empowering: Under the light of love, the seeds of sacred qualities within us burst into bloom.

Every relationship is a mirror of sorts. Yet most of the mirrors in our life merely reveal how others judge our status, prestige, wealth or physical attractiveness. Where is the mirror that can reveal our true light, and so heal our grieving soul? Where can we go to see our light reflected in the eyes of others?

Circlework is dedicated to providing such mirrors. Often, women are amazed at the way the circle helps them see themselves in a new way. Everyone— even the person they don't particularly like—has something to teach them. One participant says:

> Over and over we uncover ourselves, and it keeps going deeper. Through other women's experience we go deeper into our own. We never know what someone is going to say that will set something off in us, and allow us to learn all kinds of new things about ourselves.

At first, Amaterasu couldn't believe that the golden light she saw was truly her own. In the same way, we too may initially feel doubtful when someone holds up a mirror and says, "Look here, do you see how beautiful your light is?"

"Are they talking about me?" we think. "They must mean someone else."

VOICES FROM THE CIRCLE

We are all mingled. I see myself in other women and I see them in me. The separation disappears. I see Inge, sweet quiet Inge standing up in rage on behalf of her sister, and this incredible power that lies within her. Beautiful Anita crying, tears everywhere. Adelle fainting on the stairs. They have all become a part of me.

But our circle sisters shake their heads and say, "No. We're talking about you."

For many women, the experience of being seen through the eyes of love is new and alien. Rejection, they're familiar with. But when offered love, they may initially push it away, discount it, or doubt its sincerity. "Oh, just wait till they see my dark side," they think. When they finally decide to reveal what they consider their "bad" parts, they do so with trepidation, expecting that any second, the sharp sword of judgment will descend.

Yet in the circle, it's impossible not to notice that we all share the same kinds of thoughts, feelings, and issues. Joanne talks about this:

> I am so aware of letting out all the little secrets, being able to say the weirdest, craziest, most vulnerable things, and it really doesn't matter. As I express my thoughts and feeling, I discover that other people can relate. I can begin to stop hiding and really open up.

We are all sun goddesses who have lost sight of our own brilliance. Very few women really know their true magnificence. A thousand times, I've heard women say, "I don't have any light. *You* have light, I see it in you, but not in me."

But as their sisters hold up the great mirror, they begin to grasp the truth. "Maybe I really do have some light . . ." Slowly, they begin to venture out of their cave. And as they remember who they are, the light returns to their eyes.

Throughout the ages, mystics have described the universe as a great mirror in which the Divine searches for the reflection of its own face. In the 12th century, for example, Hildegard of Bingen heard Spirit saying to her:

> To gaze at my countenance, I have created mirrors in which I consider all the wonders of my originality, which will never cease. I have prepared for myself these mirror forms so that they may resonate in a song of praise.[1]

As if in response to God's gaze, the intelligence hidden within the heart of matter emerges, leading to the evolution of conscious life forms and ultimately of beings like Jesus or the Buddha who, like crystal-clear mirrors, show us our own ultimate potential.

We may not be enlightened, but we all have the power to serve as sacred mirrors to others. Doing so not only helps us become more confident and self-assured, but it also empowers the circle as a whole. For through the practice of sacred mirroring, we build a foundation of trust and respect that leaves us less liable to get mired in shame when our shortcomings are revealed, and more able to face them courageously. Sacred mirroring improves our chances of working with conflict in ways that lead to growth, healing and health. The fool, the child, the raging maniac—all the rejected aspects of the psyche can emerge safely in a space where our basic dignity and value are consistently honored.

VOICES FROM THE CIRCLE

So much of the shame I carried all my life is falling away. I find that whatever someone might share, I can relate to it. There is nothing new under the sun, as they say. It helps me to feel that I am not the only one who experiences certain things. No matter what it is, I am not alone.

Seeing With Sacred Eyes

This practice invites you to look at yourself and others through the eyes of love. Instead of focusing on weaknesses, your intention will be to appreciate the gifts that we all bring.

I'd suggest that you start with someone you love dearly—a friend, spouse, or child. Sit down and bring them to mind. As you meditate on them, ask yourself, "What attributes of the divine do I perceive in them?"

Examples include courage, kindness, playfulness, creativity, compassion, beauty, wildness, innocence. . . . Each of these qualities is like a unique color within the rainbow of the divine.

Usually, we don't take the time to look for the precise words that might express what we see. But naming those attributes is important because it empowers and affirms them, both within others and ourselves. Remember, whatever you see is always a reflection of what lies within you. So when you see another with sacred eyes, you are also seeing yourself anew.

Seeing with Sacred Eyes is much harder to do with people whom we dislike or are having difficulties with. However, it's extremely valuable. When we're in conflict with someone, our tendency is to focus compulsively on what we think is wrong with them. Yet when we sit down and look for the light in them, we invariably find it. This not only changes how we perceive them, it also affects the relationship. People are far more sensitive to our projections than we realize. Even if we say nothing about the shift in our perception, others will unconsciously feel it. Over the years, I've observed this so many times that I no longer doubt it.

Last but not least, *Seeing with Sacred Eyes* is a beautiful practice for couples to do together. Once the honeymoon phase is over, we tend to get lazy about expressing our appreciation. It's so easy to focus on what's wrong. But studies have shown that the relationships most likely to survive are those where people are generous in expressing their appreciation for each other. So take the time to sit down together and contemplate your beloved with sacred eyes. Even better, if he or she is willing, do it together.

CHAPTER 10

WORKING THROUGH CONFLICT

*Man must evolve for all human conflict a method which rejects
revenge, aggression and retaliation. The foundation of such a
method is love.*

Martin Luther King, Jr.

When women first form a circle, they often view it as a little slice of
heaven. Here, love reigns supreme. Nothing, they believe, will ever
disturb the idyllic sense of harmony.

Yet sooner or later, the bubble pops. Projections arise, conflict ensues, and all hell breaks loose. Anxious questioning ensues: Is this
going to destroy our circle? Are we still going to feel safe with each
other? How could this have happened? What the heck went wrong?

In most cases, nothing went wrong. The only thing "wrong," if you
want to call it that, was the expectation that the circle should be a
conflict-free zone. But if it were, how could Circlework contribute to
making a world a more peaceful place?

No. The question is not how we can prevent conflict from arising,
but rather how we can work with it in skillful and effective ways.
Nothing gives us greater hope for the future of the world than to
witness conflict being resolved carefully, caringly, and successfully.
Success, in this context, doesn't just mean that we've found a way to
get along. Success means that we all feel enriched by the process.

Conflict is like an unwelcome relative with an annoying habit of showing up on our doorstep when we least expect it. Yet as challenging as it can be, it can deepen our intimacy immensely. It provokes rich, fascinating interactions, and though it may stretch us in uncomfortable ways, the resulting expansion is real. So when conflict knocks on our door, we'd be wise to welcome it courteously and afford it the honor it deserves.

Some years ago, a conflict broke out in a long-term women's circle I was facilitating. It was a serious one, and we spent months working with it. At first, its true sources were hidden, becoming apparent only after much dialogue and soul-searching. To unravel the underlying stories and beliefs took time, energy, and a lot of patience.

Was it worth it? Absolutely. The women's eventual reconciliation evoked deep gratitude and joy because it confirmed what we all intuitively knew, but had so rarely experienced in our families and communities: that conflict need not be swept under the carpet, but can serve as a gateway to deeper and truer relationship.

What We Did

◎ We made space and time for each of the women in conflict to speak.

◎ We slowed the process down so they could speak without feeling rushed or pressured.

◎ We built in moments of silence.

◎ We made sure they really heard each other.

◎ We didn't allow them to shame or blame each other.

◎ We asked questions that helped them go deeper.

◎ We invited them to honor each other as sacred beings.

◎ We reminded them of the common center they shared as members of our circle.

◎ We gave them both plenty of love, support and appreciation.

◎ We offered a range of perspectives.

◎ We shared our own responses.

So what does reconciliation feel like? Several months after Jane and Anna resolved their conflict, I asked Jane about her experience. After thinking about the question for a minute, she said:

> Given the intensity of our conflict, I was amazed that the circle was able to help us come to a resolution. Still, for a while afterwards I didn't want to interact with Anna. It wasn't that I never wanted to talk to her again, but neither did I want to force myself into it. I still felt guarded.
>
> Well, at our last retreat, I walked in, and there she was. And to my own surprise, I felt a sense of connection and openness. For the first time since our fight we said hello, we had a conversation, and when as I was standing there talking to her, I was so aware that a shift had occurred.
>
> I thought, "What happened? This feels good." I have never experienced anything remotely like this before. I didn't even know it was possible. In my world, people just hold grudges forever.

Like Jane, most of us have never experienced conflict as a positive, creative force. Depending on how fights were handled in our family of origin, we may even equate conflict with violence. Considering the dire absence of skillful conflict resolution, both in our families and in the world, it's no wonder we tend to perceive conflict as the enemy of peace. How few of us can honestly say that our parents fought respectfully and constructively and resolved their differences in ways that satisfied them both!

Yet like it or not, conflict is part of how we grow and evolve, both as individuals and as communities. We long for harmony but often evolve in response to disharmony. We prefer to avoid

VOICES FROM THE CIRCLE

For 14 years I was part of a mom's circle. Then, it broke up. Since doing the Circlework Training I understand why it ended. We were only allowing the good stuff, we weren't allowing any conflict. So ultimately, the circle died.

tension, but the people who push our buttons and rub us the wrong way serve as yeast for our growth. If we stifle our voices in hopes of avoiding tension, what we avoid will eventually erode the integrity of the relationship.

Musicians know how out of conflicting rhythms, an entirely new rhythm can emerge. Similarly, when we make space for conflicting truths, new insights reveal themselves. Conflict is, in other words, not the opposite of peace but rather a necessary process for *maintaining* peace. Like a thunderstorm that freshens the air and renews the land, a good conflict can purify and rejuvenate our relationships.

Voices from the Circle

One of the things I came with was the belief that if she's right, I'm wrong. And If I'm right, she's wrong. Now I see that it doesn't have to be that way. I see that there is a path way that works, if we are open to it.

Of course, conflict *can* be destructive, and in our world, it often is. What prevents this, in Circlework, is that we have a strong commitment to honoring the center within each other. In other words, we view each other as sacred beings. When we argue, we do so with respect. We don't try to undermine our opponent's self-esteem. Instead, we try to listen with an open mind and heart. We approach each other, not as enemies, but as friends who share the same positive intentions, though our perspectives may differ. We don't engage in negative value judgments, for example by calling the other deceitful, cruel or unloving. We don't doubt the goodness within our opponents, but try to listen deeply and understand their feelings and views. Our goal is not to win, defeat the other, punish or to destroy them, but rather to find a solution to the problem at hand that will work for everyone. When we approach conflict in this spirit, we find that it can actually be a very beautiful and rewarding art form.

Every conflict begins with judgment, which I define as the way we justify closing our heart to someone. This shutting down of the heart is always triggered by fear. Our ego, however, is rarely willing to admit when it feels threatened. Instead, it will mask its vulnerability by insisting that others should be different than they are. If they fail to conform, we'll either cast them out of the circle of our lives or remain stuck in a toxic relationship. In some cases, we may declare them our enemies and our animosity will lead to violence.

The circle shows us an alternative. We may not like everyone we meet in the circle. However, we don't avoid them, nor do we try to change them. Instead, we simply do our best to accept them the way they are. We witness them patiently, and with curiosity, even as we witness ourselves and our responses to them. Everyone is a spiritual being, and no matter how alien their path might seem to us, they are no less valuable and necessary to the whole than we are. Therefore we try to understand their point of view, and let go of needing to make them wrong so that we can be right.

When, instead of rejecting people we don't like, we focus on trying to understand them, our perceptions often shift in amazing ways. The moment we accept them as they are, our inner contraction begins to dissolve, and the natural spaciousness of our being reasserts itself. Carol says it well:

> At times my first reaction to some people was, I don't like them. You'd mentioned up front that this might happen, and you told us that even if we disliked someone we should try to respect their core and look for the essence behind the personality. I really took that in and didn't do what I would have done in the past, which was to just shut them out. In social situations I'd be pleasant, but really I wasn't open to them.
>
> This has been an incredible experience of absorbing, listening, being patient, and making space for differences. I have learned that someone who annoyed me half an hour ago might say something truly profound or teach me something extremely valuable. Now I really love some of the people in the group whom I didn't like at first.
>
> I used to want certain people to be more spiritual or different in some way, but now I feel, no, they don't have to change for me. I feel very connected to everyone. I am seeing them differently and really accepting them and loving them the way they

are. That's so new for me. I've watched my criticism turning to understanding and affection and have discovered that on the other side of every judgment is love.

The many conflicts I've witnessed in our circles have taught me how helpful the support of a community can be when we're dealing with conflict. Alone, we may be unable to work things through, despite our best intentions. Our emotions may fly out of control. We may be unable to see the bigger picture, old habits and wounds may get in the way and prevent us from communicating skillfully. At such times, our circle can help us find a path from anger and turmoil to understanding and forgiveness. It can lovingly hold us, encourage us to express our truth, challenge us to look deeply within, and help us heal.

Most of us are not used to having our fights out in the open. We were raised to believe that we should not interfere in other people's fights, nor they in ours, and that our conflicts are none of their business. Yet when people fight, it affects the entire community, so in a sense, it really *is* their business.

When I asked Jane to speak about the role of the circle in helping her and Anna work through their conflict, she laughed and said:

God, I don't even know where to start. This was a totally new experience for me. In my family, when there was a fight, it was always hush-hush. Nobody was supposed to know that we were having problems. My parents felt ashamed so they totally isolated themselves. And that's always what I always used to do, too.

But after doing Circlework, I really get that conflict isn't just a personal problem. It affects everyone in the circle. When people fight, it hurts everyone. You know, I once heard that in certain tribal societies, when two people had a conflict, the whole tribe would stop whatever they were doing to work on the problem until harmony was restored.

Wow! That makes so much sense to me now. Our fight really did affect the whole circle, and we needed the circle to help us.

There's just no way we could have worked through this alone. Now, I really understand that there are ways of communicating that work and that can help us resolve our conflicts in a good way, a healing way. I never knew that before.

The conflict between Jane and Anna is a perfect example of why we all need what I call *relational education*—the kind that empowers us to maintain harmonious relationships. Good communication is a complex art—challenging, multilayered, and absolutely crucial to our survival as a species. While conflict resolution is merely one aspect of relational education, it's undoubtedly an extremely important one. Just look at the state of our world, and you'll see the disastrous consequences of our failure to teach and learn the art of skillful conflict resolution.

VOICES FROM THE CIRCLE

This circle has repeatedly shown me the possibility of people in the midst of conflict coming to a place of agreement. I experienced us really wanting to communicate, instead of just wanting to be right. That's so new to me.

Without relational education, we don't stand a chance at building a peaceful planetary civilization. Though we might sincerely want to serve as agents of peace, we are likely to bring discord wherever we go, simply because we were never taught the art of skillful relationship. We aren't innately more aggressive than other animals. However, we possess weapons capable of amplifying our destructive powers a million fold. Therefore we bear responsibility for bringing a higher level of consciousness to our conflicts, so that we can sow seeds of creation rather than destruction.

Every conflict I have ever witnessed in the circle has deepened my awareness of how important relational education is, and how necessary to the healing of our world. Young children need it, college students need it, and so do the elderly. In my opinion, it's a scandal that relational education isn't a key component of our educational system.

We can't single-handedly put an end to war. Still, how we deal with conflict matters, and makes a difference. We're interconnected, so every time we shift from blame to understanding, from judgment to compassion and from anger to forgiveness, we make it easier for others to do the same. Every time we replace fear and distrust with forgiveness and peace, our entire world becomes a little more peaceful.

After hearing about Jane's experience in the circle, I ask cautiously, "So do you think the world in general could get to that point of knowing how to communicate in ways that resolve conflict?"

Jane nods vigorously.

Yes, I'm sure of it. If our intention is peace, then it's possible, absolutely. In our circle, that became so clear to me. No matter what our differences are, if we are willing to be present to the other person with real respect for their place and power and truth, we can come to a place of peace. If Anna and I could do that, then so can others.

Making Peace

In separateness lies the world's great misery; in compassion lies the world's true strength.

The Buddha

When people hear that I work with Jews and Palestinians in the Middle East, their first response is often, "Oh that must be so difficult!"

Of course it *is* difficult. The wounds inflicted by personal conflicts are, after all, minor, compared to the trauma and devastation caused by the violent clashes of nations, races and ethnic groups. Those collective explosions are far more complex than the kind of disagreement that Jane and Anna were struggling with. Still, in my experience, personal and collective conflicts have something very important in common: In both cases, the key to resolution is connection.

Politicians have spent decades trying to broker a sustainable resolution to the Jewish-Palestinian conflict, to no avail. I believe their failure was predictable. Peace is, after all, not a matter of laws and political agreements but of human relationships, and to transform negative relationships, people need to meet and connect.

Sadly, in Israel and Palestine, both sides have done their best to minimize personal contact. It's understandable. After all, our knee-jerk reaction is to pull away from people we fear or distrust. A thousand years ago, this strategy probably had its merits, but in our world, it simply doesn't work. All over Israel and Palestine, you can see its bitter fruits in the form of endless barriers and boundaries, check points, walls and surveillance systems. In the long run, separation and segregation only worsen the conflict. For in the void left behind by the absence of personal contact and friendships, Ignorance deepens, fear has free reign to distort our perceptions, and enemy projections proliferate.

Of course, meeting the enemy is difficult, for a number of reasons. Obviously, it can trigger all sorts of challenging emotions such as fear, guilt, hatred, resentment and shame. By avoiding contact, we also avoid those unpleasant feelings.

Another reason why people often avoid contact with the "other" is for fear of being branded traitors by members of their own tribe. In Palestine, for example, peacemakers who seek contact with Israelis have repeatedly come under attack from their own people.

But we can observe the same patterns much closer to home. I think, for example, of Tracy, a black woman who participated in a long-term women's circle that I led. The fact that everyone else was white infuriated her friends. "What are you doing with a bunch of white folks?" they kept asking her.

But Tracy was not swayed by their disapproval. For her, Circlework was a revelation because it showed her a possibility she had never known existed: The possibility, namely, of not just finding a way to survive within a racially divided society, but of actually *healing* racism. She says:

> What this circle has taught me is that if our intention is to live to-gether in peace, then taking sides is not the answer and neither

Voices from the Circle

In the circle, I've had several experiences of getting into a conflict with someone I couldn't stand and reacted to strongly. But once we really communicated, I found we had an amazing connection, and it totally changed our relationship. This has really transformed the way I relate to people. I am learning to be courageous enough to allow this process to happen.

is choosing an ideology to live by. Instead, I want to live out of the power within me, the Spirit within, and trust it to guide me. I know it's the right choice. If people around the world could do what we're doing here, war would be a thing of the past.

Many of us aren't exactly racist or prejudiced. However, simply by avoiding those whom we feel ill at ease with, we may be unintentionally contributing to the problem. That we prefer not to venture out of our social comfort zone is quite understandable. Yet like it or not, this is precisely what we need to do today. To achieve racial healing, we need to connect across racial boundaries. It's as simple as that.

When you invite a group of people into a circle that is infused with gentleness, kindness and love, you can rest assured that they will come to appreciate each other, no matter whether they're Jews, Christians or Muslims, black, white or brown. It's natural: people are people, and what unites us is so much more powerful than what divides us. No matter how much we might disagree on certain issues, we all share the same desire to create a better future for our children and grandchildren.

When we come together in a setting where we can really hear each other and be heard, our enemy projections begin to collapse. Compassion arises naturally as we listen to each person's story and come to know their struggles and their suffering.

Regardless what the nature of the conflict we're dealing with is, and regardless of whether it affects specific individuals or entire groups, I believe that the solution always involves connection. Yet connecting through the mind alone is never enough. Above all, we need to connect through the heart. On the foundation of a strong heart connection, we can explore our differences without fear. Guilt, shame, resentment, anger, hatred—there is nothing that cannot be held in compassion when we intentionally and consistently

VOICES FROM THE CIRCLE

Circlework has helped me open to a greater diversity of people, a wider spectrum. The circle has made it intriguing, interesting, and rewarding to open to diversity, instead of fearful. I have learned that it is very important to let go of pushing for agreement and to really accept our differences. If I insist that people agree with my perspective, then our interaction becomes a power struggle. Whereas if I can really accept their position, no matter how different it is than mine, there can be space for all of us.

connect through our heart while holding the intention of fostering peace and healing.

Not everyone has the courage to encounter the "other" in open, undefended ways, as Tracy did, and as my Middle Eastern sisters do. Yet for those who have that courage, the circle is a great ally.

Peacemaking Practice

Conflict is not just something we have with other people. We also experience it internally. Most of those inner battles remain invisible. Still, they're happening, and they keep turning our inner world into a battle field. Even as we're eating that delicious brownie, we may be chastising ourselves for doing so. Or maybe, we're having an imaginary inner argument with someone else—a friend, a politician, our boss.

That's the bad news. The *good* news is that every time you notice some type of conflict within yourself, you're looking at a great opportunity to hone your skills in the art of conflict resolution.

Here are four simple steps you can use to bring peace you your inner world.

1 First, simply become aware of those inner battles. Often, we don't take this step because we aren't really paying attention to what's going on inside of us. Over the next 24 hours, try to notice every time your mind goes to war against reality. Notice the inner arguments, whether they're with yourself or with other people or situations. Notice, also, how tense your mind gets when you engage in these mini-battles. When the mind goes to war, it contracts.

2 Your next step is to identify and articulate what exactly you are waging war on. For example, you might realize:

◎ I am waging war on my body weight.

◎ I am waging war on my daughter's anger.

◎ I am waging war on my own anger.

◎ I am waging war against my despair.

3 Now, take whatever you just said and turn it around. If you said, "I am waging war against my anger," you will now say, "I accept my anger. I am willing to make peace with my anger."

Perhaps you're not really feeling it. That's perfectly okay. Say it anyway. Try it on for size. Imagine what it would feel if it were true. See if you can actually feel it physically, in your body. Do this for as long as you want, but for at least three minutes.

4 Acknowledge yourself: you are a peacemaker. No matter what happened during this exercise, it was an important step towards ending war where it matters most: Within yourself.

CHAPTER 11

Circles for Mental Health

The strongest people are not those who show strength in front of the world, but those who fight and win battles that others do not know anything about.

Jonathan Harnisch

Circlework is a highly versatile and adaptable tool that has proven its value in many environments, from prisons and hospitals to churches and boardrooms. It can be adapted to pretty much any population, as well as combined with other healing practices, such as Yoga or meditation. Of course, Circlework will look different in different environments. Yet no matter what form it takes, it always aims at creating a field of love and tapping the healing power of the circle to strengthen ourselves and our communities.

For psychotherapists, counselors, and other mental health care practitioners, Circlework is an invaluable tool. Circlework is not psychotherapy, yet it supports mental wellness by giving us an infusion of peace, contentment and joy. Moreover, it helps us stay anchored in habits and behaviors that keep us balanced and happy, even in the midst of challenging circumstances. Often, the vortex of love created in our circles is such that psychological wounds begin to heal in entirely unforced, spontaneous ways. Remember Betty, the severely depressed woman whose birthday celebration had such a dramatic impact on her mental health? Her story is just one example of how

Circlework sometimes succeeds where traditional methods have failed.

In this chapter, we're going to take a look at what Circlework might look like in an environment radically different than where my own circles are held: the acute ward of a psychiatric hospital.

Voices from the Circle

My first conscious awareness of the power of the circle came when I was working at a home for schizophrenic children. We worked with profoundly disturbed adolescents, and circles were our therapeutic tool. We had dream circles every morning. Everything was in circles. Since then I've always known that circles would always be part of my work.

For this is where Shyla, a chaplain and Circlework graduate in her fifties, leads several circles a week. Some of her circles are just for adults. Others include children above the age of twelve. Needless to say, the parameters here are quite different than in my circles. Touch, for example, is not allowed. Movement, too, is problematic, because many of the patients have trouble containing themselves.

"My natural style would be do a lot of very expansive processes," Shyla says. "But in this environment, that wouldn't feel safe. Instead, we do a lot of grounding activities. I almost always end with a process in which they imagine being a tree, firmly rooted in the ground. I'm very cautious. Their egos are extremely fragile, so my approach is very gentle."

Yet as you'll see, Shyla's circles invoke the same sense of sacredness that is the hallmark of Circlework. Here too, magic happens, and the healing that occurs is nothing short of miraculous. But I'll let Shyla speak for herself.

The people I'm working with don't see spirituality as some kind of fun, theoretical exercise. For them, it's a lifeline. They know they are not living the life they want to live, and they're more than willing to open to the possibility of connecting with Spirit as a source of real support and as a way of gaining the balance and connection they need. They talk about wanting to be kind and compassionate, yet usually they are in the psychiatric ward because they have harmed themselves or others. So we look at the disconnect.

Circlework has taught me to trust that the mentally ill have great wisdom and that they can access it, despite their condition. There's something about mental illness that cracks people open and brings them right up against questions about the nature of consciousness and their lack of control—very basic spiritual issues.

In the beginning, I often ask people to say a few words about how they are feeling. Sometimes, a paranoid person will look at me with suspicion and reply, "Why do you want to know?"

But by the end of the circle, they're really talking about things that are important to them. To them, this is not just something superficial. It's not just a game. And they are very respectful. Once in a while, someone might be sarcastic and make a flip comment, but then, someone else in the group will say, "This might not be important to you, but I need this." And they respect that, coming from a peer.

It's a locked facility. But for the most part, I use the same ground rules as we use in all our circles, such as not interrupting, listening to one another, not judging other people, not giving advice. Some people are on medication and they aren't thinking so clearly, so it's important to give them time to complete their thoughts, even if there's a long pause.

If people find it very difficult to stay in the room, they can excuse themselves and leave. They know that's all right, and they know they can come back in when they are ready. So there is a fluidity. This is very different from other circles I've been in. In the past, it always bothered me when people left. Yet here, it doesn't feel disturbing. Even if they slam the door on the way out, the circle stays intact. The membrane is permeable.

I don't think I could hold circles in this environment if I hadn't spent so much time doing Circlework and coming to the trainings. Because of that, the circle has become part of my life style. The mandala is alive within me, that is crucial. I couldn't do this work if I hadn't developed the discipline of nurturing my own spiritual life and doing the things that nurture my soul.

The head psychologist is a wonderful person, but she's very secular. She'll come out of a group and say, "Oh, wait till you get this group!" I just shrug. "Okay, thank you," I say. She can't believe what happens in our circles. All the psychologists are amazed: "How do you get them to work together like that?" I think it's because I'm so intentional about wanting it to be sacred space. I know what sacred space feels like, so Spirit can use me to create it for others.

Sometimes I have everybody name one name of the Divine. That is helpful, because it gives me a chance to talk about not judging anyone else's way and being aware that we can intentionally call in whatever gives us strength. Many people have no connection to Spirit at all, but when they see that other people do, it makes them curious.

I also invite them to pray for what they want, and usually they are comfortable with that. Not rote prayers, just to ask for what they want and open to the possibility that there might be a benevolent presence in the universe and that it might want to meet them where they are.

Not only the adults, but the kids too are very open to spirituality. They get excited about it. I don't know whether it's because of their age or what, but they seem to be more innocent and open to spiritual things.

I've definitely seen cases where it felt like someone was going through an authentic spiritual opening. We have one man who has multiple personalities. He's very bright and he has two doctorates, one in theology. He was severely abused as a child, multiple times by multiple people, and his many personalities are a creative way for him to deal with that. But he tells this story about the emergence of what he calls his spiritual self.

At the time it happened, he'd been feeling completely crazy. Then, he had an experience in which he left his body and was transported to a whole different universe. He told me, "Some people will say that I was hallucinating and delusional. But I know this came from a different place in me. While I was in that other dimension, I was told that I was creative, that I was kind, that I was loving, and that my creativity has kept me alive. I was told it was not bad that I had all these personalities." It was the first time I started to befriend myself."

He came back from that experience with compassion for all his personalities, not just the positive ones but also the angry, homicidal parts of himself. He wanted to befriend them too, because he saw that they had tried to protect him. And indeed, they had.

In Circlework, we are always holding the process as a contribution to the healing of the collective. That is something I often feel here too. In fact, people often refer to it. Many patients were severely abused, and they talk about wanting to hold what they call 'good intentions' for others who've suffered the same pain. A lot of vets come in with post-traumatic stress syndrome, and they speak of wanting to send healing energy to others who are suffering after having been in a war. It's a ripple effect.

Recently we had a 19-year-old woman who couldn't read at all, and she wanted to remember other people who can't read. She said, "I want to send good intentions to people who are like me, who aren't smart and who don't have any books." I was so touched by that. I love that they allow me to join them in such tender, vulnerable places.

There was a girl on the unit who had been a cutter and had stopped cutting. Then, another girl arrived who had also been cutting herself. It was profoundly important to this new girl to

VOICES FROM THE CIRCLE

This journey to wholeness asks us to bring our weaknesses, our doubts and fears, all the parts of ourselves that are broken, and to bless those parts. Our brokenness is another gate to our wholeness. Everything, everything counts. Our path includes everything we are and have ever done, and it's all encouraged to come into the light and to be held in love.

come to the circle and to hear the other girl's story, and hear about the choices she had made. She came to us the second day and said, "I decided I'm not going to cut myself today. I'll go to the staff if I need help. I really want to get better." And she did get better. For the time that she was there, at least, she stopped cutting.

Often at the end of a circle, I will say to them, "Look at how you've held it together for this hour." For them, holding it together for an hour is a significant thing. They didn't yell, they didn't hit anybody, they didn't attack anybody, they didn't run screaming around the room, they weren't disrespectful, they didn't take their clothes off . . .

One day, I asked them to think of a time they felt real joy. There was a woman there who had taken a severe overdose and was extremely depressed. This woman said, "I remember when I was in high school and I got a part in a musical, *The Sound of Music*. I remember what it was like to stand there . . ."

Then she started to walk around the room, telling us about the experience, and what she wore, and how the cast of that musical became the family she didn't have at home. And by the time she got finished telling the story, her face was shining.

Somebody said, "Look at her! Look at her face!" And she started laughing, and everybody else started laughing too. They recognized that in the recounting of that moment, she was there again. So that's a great way you can teach people to get in touch with their joy. You don't have to sit on a mat for seven years and meditate. We were all transported, we were all right there with her in that moment.

The sad thing is that once they get discharged, they no longer have a circle. It's hard to find in our society. Those with addictions can go to AA meetings, but that's not for everyone. I think sometimes people come back to the unit because they miss the circle. It becomes a home, a sanctuary. Offering them a circle outside of the unit might cut back on some of that. Some people cry when they leave the unit. Often, they are going back to situations that are not good.

There's so much compassion in the people I work with. We had a little boy of 12, which is the youngest you can be on our unit, and there were three older kids on the unit who were 15, 16 and 17. The 12-year-old was autistic, severely disabled, really not able to relate to anybody at all. He was in his own world, doing a lot of repetitive motion. It was very sad to see. He was also very disruptive and couldn't participate.

But then the older kids started taking care of him. It was beautiful to watch. One day, they wanted him to come and be in the circle. So he entered the room but not the circle, and he was mussing with stuff and being disruptive. I tried to talk to him and invite him in. But he didn't know me, so it was useless.

Then, one of the girls got up. She went over and took him by the hand and said, "Now Jimmy, you have to come over here, and you're going to sit right here between me and Laura, and John is going to be right there, and this is Jacquie, and she's okay. So he sat down with them.

Then the girl looked around and said, "Now what do we know he likes?" And they all said, "He likes to color!"

I'm just sitting there, watching this all unfold. So they got him crayons and paper, and every time he got disruptive, one of them would come over and sit with him and show him what he could do with the crayons.

These kids are all in there because they are suffering from acute psychiatric illness. But they were so gentle with him and so skillful. I was amazed. They knew what to do, they knew when to do it, and even as they were caring for him, they were also able to continue participating in the circle. They gave that boy so much compassion.

At the end of the circle, the older boy, whose name was John, said to the other kids, "Why do you think God created him like that? Why does he have to live like this? This is terrible."

There was a long pause. Then, very quietly, one of the girls said, "Well, just look what he does for us!"

Wow, I thought. John looked at the girl and said, "Yes, I guess that's true."

They were so kind to each other, and yet they were there because they've been beating the crap out of someone at their school, or something of that sort. But I know that next time they see a kid being disruptive, they'll remember Jimmy, and they'll say, "Maybe I can't help this kid, but at least I'm not going to trip him. I'm not going to make fun of him, because I know someone like that."

The longer I'm here, the more I think the word "normal" should be just left out of the dictionary. There is no such thing. The pain of the world is no theory to them. They know what it's like to be hurting, and to be rejected by others who view them as a problem.

CHAPTER 12

MAKING SPACE FOR GRIEF

What is often diagnosed as depression is actually low-grade chronic grief locked into the psyche, complete with the ancillary ingredients of shame and despair. . . . This refusal to enter the depths has shrunk the visible horizon for many of us, dimmed our participation in the joys and sorrows of the world. We suffer from what I call premature death—we turn away from life and are ambivalent toward the world, neither in it nor out of it, lacking a commitment to fully say yes to life.

Francis Weller[1]

I believe we all need a place where we can cry to our heart's content, and where our grief can be acknowledged, honored, and held in community. Grief is an important emotion. Not an easy one, but it's how we digest the experience of loss and transform it into something that has depth and meaning. Grief gives us what the Quakers call "gravitas," a Latin word meaning "gravity" or "weight"—the good kind of weight that turns us into true elders. People who have owned and transformed their grief are like heavy boulders that can stand unmoved in the midst of hurricanes, providing shelter and refuge to others.

When a woman comes to a circle, and finds it to be a place of true kindness that welcomes her authentic self-expression, her tears may naturally begin to flow. The dam that has been holding them back crumbles, and she experiences what some would call a break-down, but what is actually a break-through. Don't get me wrong, Circlework is not an inherently heavy or sad process by any means. There's lots of laughter and play. But life invariably includes suffering and loss, and in our society, there are few places where we can receive the support we need to move through our grief.

Of course, we're capable of grieving alone. But it's better—much better—if we can share our grief with others. When our grief is held in the bowl of the circle, we can allow ourselves to let go, trusting that our sisters won't let us drown in our tears, but will help us re-emerge into the light.

VOICES FROM THE CIRCLE

I feel a deep well of grief in me. Sometimes it feels like I'm holding the world's sorrow. It feels so huge. But in this circle, I can let it have a place.

I remember well the sunny morning when Sharon, a heavy-set woman in her fifties, grieved for her broken marriage. For a long time, she sobbed inconsolably while we held and rocked her. Later, exhausted, she rested quietly in the center of our circle as we gently cradled her head, held her hands, and tenderly laid hands on her heart. For several minutes, there was no sound other than birdsong pouring in through the open windows.

Finally, Sharon opened her clear blue eyes and looked at us. Once again, I was struck by the way tears can wash away years of tension from our faces, leaving them as soft and open as a child's. And to my delight, I saw a little smile begin to curl around Sharon's face, as if the sun were peeping out from behind clouds. Like a circle of mirrors, we smiled back at her.

And then, ever so slowly, her smile broadened into a grin that grew larger and larger until suddenly, her large body began to shake with laughter, seized by a force against which all resistance was useless. It was a beautiful thing to see such joy overtaking a person who just a few moments ago had been mired in deep grief. Her laughter was infectious, and before we knew it, we all were rolling on the floor, roaring with laughter at the wild, crazy, terrible beauty of life.

Circlework can be intense and emotionally challenging. All the more reason to welcome the untamable laughter that shakes us loose and reconnects us with our wild, ecstatic freedom. I always view it as a good sign when women feel safe enough to drop their guard and become playful and foolish. Sacred space doesn't need to be serious and solemn. Laughter is a good medicine that helps us shed the heaviness and gloom that overtake us when we take life's dramas too seriously.

There's one kind of silliness that signals embarrassment or boredom. There's another that swoops down on us like an angel of mirth after we have descended into the depths of our soul, spoken our truth and wailed our grief. A great sense of relief may arise then, as if a heavy boulder had been lifted from our souls. We feel light and giddy with joy.

Someone starts to giggle for no reason at all, and laughter begins to ripple from belly to belly like wildfire. No way to contain it, no way to repress it. It dies down, only to start anew, a healing fire that leaps and licks across the circle until everyone is left exhausted, with tear-streaked faces, loose bellies, and warm, contented hearts.

When this happens, I know the spirit of healing is among us. We have come through the dark valley and back out into the light.

Trusting the Flow

The heart that breaks open can contain the whole universe.
Joanna Macy

Once, in a circle that included both men and women, I gave everyone a piece of clay and asked them to hold it while imagining that the clay was their own body. Within seconds, a man in his late fifties called Andrew began to weep. Later, he said:

> It has something to do with the quality of this space. Everything is so slow here, so gentle, and as I slow down I am beginning to become conscious of my pain and to feel it with awareness. I've been denying my feelings and escaping into work. Here, I can't do that.

Spend time in circles, and you'll realize how much pain many people hide beneath a façade of cheerfulness. They come to the circle wanting to become visible, but also wanting to hide because, to some degree, they feel ashamed of their pain.

Janet used to be one of them: "In my old life, if someone asked me how I feel right now, I'd say, fine. I'm so used to hiding and pretending I'm okay. But I'm *not* fine. It's important to let myself say that, without judging myself."

Of course, it would not be smart to reveal our suffering indiscriminately. We need discernment as to when to wear our armor, and when to take it off. But many people *never* take their emotional armoring off. They live in it, they sleep in it, and they even make love in it.

That's not a comfortable or healthy way to live. Yet what other option is there when we don't have places where it's safe to let down our guard and become visible, emotionally as well as physically? Sadly, emotional loneliness is not the exception but the norm in our society.

In daily life, we often repress our tears because we consider them a sign of weakness. Yet actually, tears usually mean that we are softening and opening. Like snowmelt in spring, they signal that some inner kernel of hardness is dissolving. We speak of "breaking down", as if crying were a sign of weakness and defeat. Yet more often than not, our tears signal a victory over a lifetime of conditioning that tells us to hide our true feelings.

When we believe that certain emotions are good, others bad, we'll naturally try to dam the flow of the "bad" emotions. In fact, there is no such thing as a good or a bad emotion. Anger and joy, grief and fear are all the same substance manifesting in different ways. Anger is hot and fast-moving, while grief is deep and watery. Both are energy formations—energy clouds, you might say, or swirls of color, eddies in the river. Set them free to flow and they will transform into something else. Just as a river rafter learns how water moves, and how to relate to the currents, so Circlework helps us get more comfortable with the flow of our emotions. We learn not to fear the turbulence but to trust that eventually, we'll pass into calmer waters.

Emotions that can't flow can't transform. Instead, they gradually freeze in place like sheets of ice. Many of us have little icebergs in certain corners of our hearts that have not budged in decades, and that won't melt until the warm sun of compassion shines on them. Approach them with judgment or self-loathing, and they just freeze up tighter.

The compassion of a circle is like a fire that causes those numb, frozen places to thaw. As trust builds, we may begin to express feelings we may never have felt safe enough to reveal before. Something in us allows this because it recognizes grief as a portal to joy. Feeling is feeling; you cannot have the light without the dark. Push away your pain, and your joy will vanish with it.

We're all part of a great dance of energy. The question is, do we trust the dance? Do we trust where it leads us? For many people, the initial answer is no. They don't let their body move because they're afraid of looking foolish. They don't let their voice out because they sense that their voice is like a cork—let it pop, and who knows what else might come bubbling out. . . . They don't express their anger because they worry they might turn violent. They don't let out their fear because it might be too overwhelming. They don't let out their grief because they might drown in it. Some people don't let out any emotion at all, because they consider emotionality a sign of weakness. When asked to join the dance, they shake their heads. "Thanks, but no."

In Circlework, we respect the no. After all, nobody else can tell, the way we ourselves can, whether we're ready to open up or not. Nobody else is qualified to decide when the time is right.

Still, we *do* need encouragement. It's important to be invited to the dance, and to know that when we're ready, we'll be welcomed. For the time being, we might just need to watch. This period of watching is important preparation. It might look like we're just sitting there doing nothing, when in fact, we may be restructuring our whole belief system and preparing for our own break-through.

VOICES FROM THE CIRCLE

I am truly blessed. And still, I wake up in the morning shaking. The world situation affects me all the time. I'm very conscious of it even though I hardly ever speak about it.

Collective Grief

Today, many of us are feeling an aching, inconsolable grief for the world—for the decimated forests and the poisoned rivers, for the children orphaned by war, for the whales and the polar bears.

I shall never forget the sight of Asha, a strong, tall woman with long black hair, standing in the center of our circle, tears streaming down her face. As we watched in silence, we saw a power gather in her body until it condensed and rose up like lava from the core of her being, pouring out through her mouth in an anguished wail so penetrating it seemed to crack open the sky.

Clearly, she was wailing not for herself alone but for all of us—for the human race, for our lost innocence and for the ravaged beauty of the planet. This was no cry of weakness or helplessness. Though born of suffering, it was an outpouring of unshakeable strength, the kind of strength that comes when one is crying for the sake of all beings.

We all know our planet is wounded. However, I suspect that women tend to hold this knowledge in a somewhat different way than men do. I would describe it as a more cellular way, meaning that often, women's pain seems to erupt directly out of their bodies. At times, their conscious mind seems to be the last organ in their body to realize the depth of their grief.

Officially, such grief is dismissed as invalid and unfounded. Don't we have everything we need? Aren't we housed and well fed?

Consumer society has stripped the human heart of its dignity and reduced it to something that is supposed to be satisfied with sentimental movies and piles of toys. Yet we are bigger than that, and we need a bigger kind of happiness.

Just like the individual psyche, the collective psyche too has a will to heal itself. When certain feelings have been insufficiently acknowledged, pressure builds and eventually surfaces wherever it can—usually in the hearts and minds of those who are energetically sensitive

VOICES FROM THE CIRCLE

How much longer can the earth stand what we're doing? How can we sustain our world if we're destroying the basic rhythms of nature? I don't often go there. I can't afford to go into a place of depression. I've got to hold a place of hopefulness in the work I do. But I'm wondering.

and permeable. They are the ones who as children were told that they were "too sensitive" because they cried inconsolably for the deer lying dead by the side of the road, or for the little boy next door who had no father.

If you are strongly affected by the state of our world, you must find a way to accept, channel and make peace with your grief, anger and fear. Otherwise, you are liable to get sick, for unconscious emotional pain often expresses itself in the form of physical ailments. Today, growing numbers of people struggle with states of dis-ease that reflect the unacknowledged distress of the collective.

Some women take their grief for the planet to a psychotherapist. But psychotherapy may not offer them the support they need. Typically, the therapeutic model approaches suffering as an individual problem. Yet aren't grief and rage perfectly sane responses to an insane world? What we need is not to be "fixed," but to be invited into a sanctuary where our emotions can flow and wind their way back to the ocean of power from where they came. By creating spaces where our collective pain can be expressed and honored, we claim our power to heal it.

The problems seem so huge, and sometimes we feel so helpless and impotent. We are, in fact, by no means helpless. Yet in order to effect real transformation, we must not only acknowledge the problems but also find ways of taking care of ourselves in the process. This means, among other things, being prepared to hold and heal the emotions that rise up. If we can't find a way to comfort each other in our pain, hold each other in our fear, and guide each other through our rag, then our emotions will immobilize us. When, on the other hand, we give them space to flow, we find we that stagnation transforms into fresh insight, helpless rage into fierce determination and grief into compassion.

The more our society insists on denying the seriousness of the crisis, the more suffering this creates for those who cannot help but feel our collective pain. As long as our pain is dismissed as a symptom of personal pathology, we are bound to feel unheard and unseen at a deep level. The circle cannot change the realities of our times, It can, however, provide a sanctuary where we can express and share our pain. By creating such spaces, Circlework opens the doors for us to claim the power we truly do have, but can't access in isolation.

Paradoxically, this journey of embracing our pain for the world leads not to greater despair but to hope. As one woman said after practicing Circlework for several years, "My life is bigger and less isolated. I am less fearful in the midst of world events that I find utterly terrifying. I find myself with a kind of freedom and hope that would have been impossible before."

Circlework in Times of Crisis

In our day and age, events that plunge entire communities into states of chaos, such as hurricanes, floods, wars, or terrorist attacks, have become increasingly common. Under these conditions, it's especially important that we learn the basics of skillful circle facilitation. When our world is falling apart, coming to a nurturing circle can be profoundly comforting. What's happening is scary, and most of us don't want to be alone when we're scared. Instead, we crave that basic, instinctual sense of protection and reassurance that a loving circle can provide.

In times of crisis, circles can also help us sort through the chaos within our own hearts and minds and gain some clarity on where we stand. Since time immemorial, people have used circle gatherings to create a vortex, a portal through which wisdom can enter. In turbulent situations, it's especially important that do this. Otherwise, our actions and responses are liable to come from a place of fear-fueled reactivity. By dancing, praying, and talking together within the sacred field of the mandala, we can access storehouses of strength and resilience, courage and insight that would otherwise remain inaccessible.

Sadly, crisis often comes hand-in-hand with trauma. This, too, is a reason to call a circle when times are rough. Circles have a great capacity to heal trauma, not in the way of modern psycho-therapy, but by applying more primeval, ancient medicines used by tribal peoples around the world. To heal trauma, we begin by invoking the spirit of the mandala. We hold the traumatized person in a bowl of love, faithfully, and for as long as it takes. We ask for healing on their behalf, honor who they are and listen to their stories with an open heart.

Ron's Circle

Although I myself lead mainly women's circles, men too need to be held in the embrace of a caring circle. Women have far more permission to cry when they're sad, or to admit when they're scared. For men, it's not so easy. Few men have safe places where they can open up emotionally and reveal their vulnerability, without worrying about being ridiculed or judged as weak. In the absence of such havens, numbness easily becomes their default mode.

This is especially true of men who've been traumatized by violence or warfare. When they lack places where they can find healing and renewal, darkness and desolation can easily overtake them. Currently, many veterans, for example, have no way of processing what happened to them. Returning from places like Iraq or Afghanistan, they carry the war inside of them. Many are disillusioned and confused. Some who seek psychological counseling get mired in red tape. Others don't even try.

Within every trauma lies a potential initiation. Yet we all bear responsibility for holding the members of our community in compassion as they follow the difficult and perilous passageway to rebirth.

What if we offered veterans a place where they could tell their stories in the presence of a community committed to respectful, compassionate listening? What every one of them had such a circle?

There's no doubt the healing that such circles could facilitate would benefit all of us.

Voices from the Circle

It's hard for me to cry. But in the circle, tears come up because I'm touched so deeply. It isn't necessarily that something is sad. It's just that everyone's truth is so touching, especially when it connects with my own. It's the authenticity that melts my defenses.

At this point in time, women's circles are far more numerous than men's, and good male circle leaders are far and few between. However, they do exist. One of them is Ron, a teacher and counselor in his fifties. Ron knows, from his own experience, how crucial it is that men have places where they can lay down their grief and be held in the love of a caring circle.

Listening to his hearty laughter, it's hard to imagine that he was once angry and cynical. Yet he assures me that indeed, he was. "In my 20s I was a bitter young man," he says. "Bitter and full of rage. I could easily have ended up in jail."

"So what changed you?" I ask.

Without hesitation, he says, "My circle. Without it, I doubt I'd still be alive today."

Ron's circle was an ongoing group that included about 25 people. Here, he felt accepted and safe. He didn't need to put up a façade or pretend to be anything other than what he was. The group had been meeting every other week for about three years when something happened that would change Ron's life forever.

Ironically, the event occurred at a meeting that Ron almost missed. "I was in a really pissy mood," he remembers. "I was angry and irritated. I was laying blame and finding fault with everybody and everything."

However, at the last minute, Ron decided to attend the meeting despite his foul mood.

As usual, the process began with a check-in: One by one, everyone shared how they were feeling.

Often, we think we know beforehand what we're going to say when our turn to speak comes. But then, we may find, as we listen within, that something entirely different wants to be expressed. That's how it was for Ron on that fateful day. He thought he knew what he was going to say—something like, "Well, I'm feeling pissed off right now, all these things are bugging me."

But when the moment came, he hesitated. Somehow, he knew that what he'd planned to say wasn't the whole truth. Something else was going on. But what? He wasn't sure.

So, instead of speaking, he just sat there in silence and looked around the circle. Instead of pushing people away, as his mood would have him do, he decided to let them in. One by one, he looked them in the eye, and one by one, he saw that they were utterly present with him, and that he was held in a strong, unwavering circle of kindness.

We all know how good it feels when a single friend gives us their full, undivided attention. Now, imagine that experience magnified a hundredfold, and you get a sense of the healing power that is generated when an entire circle holds one individual in their loving attention. The energetic impact is tremendous.

No doubt, Ron's friends could see that he was in pain. When we care about someone, we want to help. This is natural. We want to fix their problems. But in the circle, we curb that impulse. After all, we can't take away another's pain. All we can do is hold the person in our compassion. Compassion is like a golden light that shines through our hearts. In a circle, those individual lights fuse into a single golden ring. Then, the circle becomes a sacred bowl capable of holding just about anything. So it was in Ron's circle. Nobody told him what to do, nobody offered any comments or advice. They simply held him in compassion.

Holding is healing—intuitively, we all know this. When we bang our elbow, we cup it with our hand. When a baby bumps its head, we place our hand over the bruise to "make it better." Emotional pain, too, needs to be held in the cupped hand of our compassionate attention. Attention is a state of pure, unadulterated presence and perhaps most fundamental form of love.

Of course, it's a two-way street: Others can't hold us in compassion unless we are willing to let them see who we really are, and what we're experiencing. This is why in our circles, we try to speak as honestly as

VOICES FROM THE CIRCLE

The circle is a home for my tears. It seems that I could cry forever here, but these are not tears of sadness but of joy, sorrow, fullness, love, beauty—everything. I don't cry enough. The circle is a safe, protected place where I can allow it to happen.

we can. Our truth is the only offering we can make that has any real value.

At first, Ron held back. Yet eventually, something deep inside began to melt. Like sheets of ice, his anger began to dissolve and slip away, and his true feelings started welling up, flooding his eyes with tears:

> I just fell onto the floor sobbing. It was grief, grief for all the people I had lost to AIDS. I am gay, and throughout the 80s, I'd watched friends and lovers die, without any mention from the federal government that there was even a problem. To them, there wasn't a problem because they believed only gay men were affected. Meanwhile, 35 to 40 people whom I had loved and had been close to had died of the disease.
>
> I was enraged about it, really enraged. I got involved in an AIDS project, but really, I was just steeling myself with rage. As long as I stayed totally focused on my anger, I was able to push the grief away. That grief was so huge that I couldn't have gotten anywhere near it on my own. But when I came to the circle and looked into people's eyes, it began to surface. That circle held me both psychologically and spiritually in a way that made it possible for me to start the grieving process that I'd been avoiding for ten years.
>
> If it hadn't been for that circle, I don't know where I'd be today. Probably dead. It was definitely a pivotal experience that put me on the path I'm still on today. Having experienced the healing power of the circle, I became determined to share it with others. So that's what I've been doing ever since.

Ron's experience is not unusual. Countless times, I've seen how within minutes after a circle starts, people start to express feelings they didn't even know they had.

Our minds view certain thoughts and feelings as dangerous and try to avoid them. Yet some other part of us—call it the soul, if you will—wants to be whole, and is always on the look-out for opportunities for healing. When we enter a sacred circle, its ears perk up like those of a cat at the sound of a can-opener.

"I am here," the circle whispers to us. "You are held in love. You are safe." And suddenly, we find ourselves saying yes to the birthing of consciousness and yes to the surrender that Spirit is asking of us.

Blessing the Men

Do you know any men who, like Ron, have had the courage to embrace their pain and vulnerability? If you do, inwardly send them your thanks and gratitude. They are the pioneers who are helping us build a new, more peaceful world.

Now imagine a young man who has never done this, and who associates vulnerability with weakness and shame. Sit down and write him a letter. What would you want him to know? What could you say that might help him embrace his fears and his tears?

CHAPTER 13

Honoring the Body

I've been in many other groups, but Circlework has an altogether
different foundation. In those groups, only words were used. In
our circle, there are so many other elements that create incredible
depth—the touching, the poetry, the music, the silence.

Many spiritual and psychological group processes pay little attention
to the physical body. In Circlework, however, we honor the body as a
sacred vehicle and a source of wisdom. We dance, stretch, and breathe,
we touch and are touched. We take time to listen to our bodies and let
their wisdom inform us. A circle where people just sit for hours on end
is definitely not engaged in Circlework. A Circlework leader, I would
add, needs no special training in dance or body therapies. She need
only be committed to creating safe spaces where we can listen to our
bodies and honor their wisdom. In our society, such places can be difficult to find.

In daily life, we often force our body to match the frenzied pace
of the thought-addicted mind. In our circles, we do the opposite:
Through breath, movement, touch and sound, we slow down the
mind until it matches the rhythms of nature. As the tangled web of
thought dissolves, we tap into deeper sources of wisdom and guidance. Stress and tension melt away as we come home to the present
moment, to the earth, and to our own embodied truth. We all know

that our bodies need sleep, nutrition, exercise and rest. Yet I am convinced, no matter how much Western medicine might deny it, that they also need spiritual nourishment. Beauty, gentleness and tenderness are as medicinal as Vitamin B and C.

Of course, we all know how helpful it is to inhabit a healthy, relaxed body. It's hard to live happily in a body that's in pain. But tending to our bodies is also an essential step towards creating a more peaceful world. Our body is part of the earth, so the way we treat our body is a reflection of how we treat the earth. How shall we live sustainably on this earth, if we can't live sustainably in our own bodies? By calling us home to our bodies, Circlework calls us home to the earth.

Do we criticize and reject our body, or do we lovingly appreciate it? How well are we willing to care for it? What would it mean to really respect it?

We cannot be peacemakers in the world if we're at war with our own body. And let's face it, many if not most women are. As women, we're not supposed to get fat or old. We not supposed to be affected by our hormones. We're not supposed to need as much rest as we do. We're not supposed to look the way we look. Simply put, most of us feel that our bodies are not okay. We might not want to give ourselves such negative messages, but how to stop?

Circlework can help. Of course, it can't undo all the damage inflicted by an insane culture. However, it can give us an alternative experience of ourselves as vessels of sacred life force. When we dance in the circle, we do so, not in hopes of burning off calories, but for the pure pleasure of it. Here, rest is not only permitted but encouraged. Slowing down is equated, not with slacking off but with coming to our senses.

Being present in the body can take courage. Instead of avoiding our pain, despair, and exhaustion, we must be willing to experience our vulnerability and mortality in a direct, undefended way. Yet the

VOICES FROM THE CIRCLE

I've had issues with accepting my body. The touch I've experienced in the circle has helped me a lot with that. When you are touched lovingly, as by a mother, within a safe container, it sends a very powerful message of acceptance.

rewards far outweigh the challenges. By dropping from identification with thought into the mysterious realm of the body, we're choosing aliveness over numbness and connection over disassociation. We are, in other words, reclaiming our capacity, not only for pain but also for pleasure, joy and ecstasy.

Voices from the Circle

The touching exercise we did was a real turning point for me. It was delightful. A whole layer of tension fell off, and today I feel much more open and present than I did. I like being here a lot. Being touched and cradled by women in that nurturing way is something I never had.

Personally, I believe that for women, this commitment to fully embodying ourselves is our portal to power. I can't speak for men. But as a woman, my sense of self is inextricably entwined with my experience of living in a body. What my body looks like from the outside is not the point. Whether it conforms to the beauty standards of my society is irrelevant. What matters is my own inner experience of being present in the here and now. If I am to be happy, and to know my own sacredness, it must happen right here, within this temporary and fragile body.

When a woman embodies herself fully and shamelessly, she becomes a priestess—not in the religious sense, but in the sense that she honors her inner world as her temple and takes responsibility for ensuring that it's well tended and cared for. Just as a priestess purifies her temple and invites the sacred presence, so an empowered woman tends to her inner sanctuary.

You too can call on your inner priestess to help take care of yourself. She knows how to create an energy field that feels sacred, authentic and healing. She can help you chose the books you read, the music you listen to, the forms of physical exercise you do, and the friends you spend time with. She knows what kind of food your body needs and what environments it finds healing. In the midst of life's dramas, she can give you the courage to be present in your body.

Your inner priestess is fiercely committed to creating the kind of world where you would *want* to be fully present and embodied. Needless to say, this is also the kind of world you would want for your children and grandchildren. She is, in other words, both an activist and a spiritual seeker, a pragmatist and a mystic.

Touch

In Circlework, we use a wide range of practices to connect with our body. In the *Circlework Training Manual*, you can find detailed instructions for many of them. Here, I will merely briefly highlight a few of the main tools that we work with and that you, too, can use to connect to the wisdom of your body and of Mother Earth.

The first is touch. You're already familiar with the Heart Greeting—one of many Circlework practices that involves physical touch. For those who are uncomfortable with the idea of touching and being touched by complete strangers, I often provide a touch-free option. Yet in the end, most don't avail themselves of it. They seem to sense that the circle is a safe environment, and afterwards, they often remark on how good it felt to be touched in caring, non-sexual ways.

Touch is an incredibly powerful healing tool. It can relieve fear, soothe pain, and restore our sense of wholeness, sending a message of love from one heart to another. And in the circle, touching and being touched feels safe. Even people who initially can't imagine allowing themselves to be touched by someone other than an intimate partner or a massage therapist usually change their minds within short order.

"We Midwesterners are not much into touch," one woman acknowledged:

> There are tons of jokes about the stoic Lutherans, and to a large extent, they're true. My parents were loving but not particularly physical. We hug hello and good-bye, and that's about it. So when I came to the circle, I wasn't used to being touched, and at first, it freaked me out. But the practice of touch is built into the structure of this work, and it has been very nurturing to me. In the circle, touch comes from the heart, and there's a freedom and safety to open your heart and not be guarded.

VOICES FROM THE CIRCLE

I want to express my gratitude to you for the way you held me in our last meeting. It was a profound experience. In my family, no one ever gave me that kind of nurturing, not even my mother, and I came to believe that I would never receive what I had missed. To some extent I was nurtured by therapy. But the experience in our circle is so much more primal. I feel it throughout my body, that nurturing and tenderness and deep acceptance. I've been longing for this for a long, long time, but I never believed I could have it. And after I went home, it didn't leave—I still felt carried by the circle, by you.

Ilse, a lady in her seventies, wept as she told us that in our circle, she'd been touched for the first time since the death of her husband over 14 years ago. Like Ilse, millions of elderly men and women are never held, stroked, or touched. The situation is all the more tragic for being completely unnecessary, for to give the gift of touch is easy and natural. Most people love to nurture others. All they need is a container where they feel safe enough to do so honestly, openly, and authentically. A circle can provide a structured environment where we can give and receive touch without fearing that we'll be misunderstood as making sexual advances.

What scares people most about touch, however, is actually not the association with sex. Rather, it's the fact that touch can evoke emotions. We might speak at length about a loss we suffered, but it's only when someone lays a gentle hand on our shoulders that our tears begin to flow.

"Well," you may be thinking, "I'm not into all that touchy-feely stuff. I'm not comfortable touching strangers, let alone spilling my guts in their presence."

In a culture where coolness and numbness are the default mode, sharing feelings can indeed feel uncomfortable. But then, we don't come to the circle to be comfortable. We come to heal and to grow, both personally and spiritually. And for this to happen, we need to open up. The fact is, we rarely change because of what we *think*. We're far more likely to change because of what we *feel*. As a motivator, nothing comes close to the power of emotion.

As long as we remain stuck in our heads, we can talk for days on end about our issues and nothing will change. We'll go home, and everything will be exactly the same. For change to happen, we need to get in touch with the truths that live in our heart and belly, and be willing to let others see who we really are.

I would encourage you, therefore, to become just a little more shameless in matters of the heart. Let people come just a little bit closer. Try opening up just a little bit more. Question your beliefs about

Voices from the Circle

My body feels like a safe container in a way it never has before. The circle feels so solid and safe, and it has put me in touch with the integrity of my body, the way it really supports me and my journey.

what emotions it's okay to feel, and when, and with whom.

When we speak of feeling "touched," we acknowledge that touch is not just skin-deep. Rather, the touch of a gentle, caring hand can reach all the way to our heart. It can give us that extra bit of support we need to allow what lies within us to emerge, no matter what it might be.

This might seem like a small thing, but it is not. For as Jesus says in the Gospel of Thomas, "If you bring forth what is within you, what you bring forth will save you. If you do not bring forth what is within you, then what you do not bring forth will destroy you."

Music and Dance

In most indigenous societies, people danced regularly. We, on the other hand, do so only rarely. Personally, I believe it's a lack that affects us far more than we commonly realize. We *need* to dance—it's part of our genetic make-up. Dance isn't just a form of entertainment, it's a powerful medicine. Without it, we get tense. We worry too much, get depressed and feel less attractive. We aren't nearly as much fun to be around as we might be. When a community acknowledges and honors dance as a basic need, everyone benefits.

> **VOICES FROM THE CIRCLE**
>
> The music, the dancing, the singing. . . . They all alter my consciousness. Talk is such a small part, in the end.

Music and Dance . . .

◎ Nourish body, heart, and soul.

◎ Bond communities.

◎ Bring us into harmony with nature.

◎ Connect us to Spirit and to the healing forces of the universe.

"But," some will object, "I don't like to dance!" Granted, not everyone does. Nor do they need to; in Circlework, nobody is ever pressured

Voices from the Circle

I used to be terrified of dance. No way was I going to make a fool of myself in front of other people. It's such a gift that now, I am able to move freely. I no longer worry whether people are looking at me or whether I am doing it right. Now, when I hear the music, it goes right into my body and I start to move. When we move, I feel very connected to myself and to everyone in the circle.

I sometimes get so caught up in my mind, and then I can't find the right words to express what I'm feeling. But after we've worked with movement, the words seem to flow easily from a place of centeredness.

to engage in any activity. If they prefer not to participate, that's fine.

However I'm convinced, based on what I've seen, that far more people really like to dance than we ordinarily assume. Initially, they might feel awkward, self-conscious or embarrassed. But in the circle, those feelings usually change quickly. Often, by the end of our time together, participants who initially described themselves as non-dancers declare that, from now on, they intend to dance at every opportunity.

What made them change their minds? Quite simply, they were encouraged to move exactly the way they wanted. Once they realized that nobody was going to judge them, laugh at them or tell them they were doing it wrong, they started to relax. Their inhibitions weakened, their comfort level grew and they discovered how pleasurable and healing movement can be. Maybe it didn't look like anything much from the outside. No matter, the inner experience was no less healing and sacred. One woman comments:

> I use to feel very inhibited around movement, but dancing in the circle has given me a whole new sense of freedom. For me, it's been very helpful that we often move with our eyes closed. How we look has no part of it. It's all about how it feels within, and about the internal pleasure of moving and feeling the music in the body. That's what's emphasized. The whole social mask associated with dancing in a club or at a party is completely out of the picture.

To move, without trying to control the flow of energy, is an immensely healing experience. Young children know this, and never worry what they look like. All they care about is how they feel from the inside. But somewhere along the line, many people decide that how they look is more important than how they feel. What will others think? Will they look klutzy, or slutty, or plain foolish?

Perhaps you too are afraid of making a fool of yourself. But you know what? *It doesn't matter.* You can choose to stay small, or you can set yourself free—it's entirely your choice. Why should you care what others think? It's not important. What is important—very much so—is whether or not you experience the total aliveness of which you're capable. To sacrifice that possibility would be a tragic loss. One woman comments:

> For me, movement is a way of getting in touch with my power. It gets me out of my head and into my body, so I can be grounded and in touch with earth energy. It's truly ecstatic. And I think this is true for a lot of women. Of course the movement we do in the circle is nothing like aerobics or like some sort of formal dance. It's very soulful and sacred. I can just go places within myself and become a vessel for whatever's running through me. I always feel beautiful when I do that.

Around the world, dance and music come hand in hand. Indeed, in my eyes, a circle without music would be like a bird without wings. Many types of circles don't use music at all, but in Circlework, it's an essential element of the process.

As a universal language, music speaks directly to our hearts of beauty, joy, suffering, and redemption. It can comfort the grieving, give hope to the hopeless, and soften the hardest of hearts. In comparison, words are clumsy things—awkward, rough-edged, and fraught with potential for misunderstanding. Music can guide us into sacred space, calm our busy mind and encourage our heart to soften and open. It can soothe and heal, inspire and awaken us. It can unite us in a common rhythm. It can awaken love, longing and joy.

Besides incorporating Western music in my circles, I also use music from India, Persia, Tibet, Mali—you name it. There's nothing like world music for helping us feel connected to the global community. With its rich and diverse beauty, world music assures us that what we're trying to accomplish is indeed possible. For in the realm of music, the creation of a peaceful global

VOICES FROM THE CIRCLE

Once I went to a jazz festival right after a Circlework retreat. I got up and danced with my eyes closed. I was still filled with that amazing sense of freedom and abandon we'd shared in the circle, and so thrilled to be in this beautiful spot listening to live music. When I opened my eyes, a little circle of people had gathered around to watch. Someone came up and said, "So, are you a dancer? You must be a dancer." Wow! You have to understand that I have felt really, really awkward for much of my life. Previously, no one would ever have thought I was a dancer. But now, when I move, my soul moves through me, and I feel beautiful.

I sometimes get so caught up in my mind, and then I can't find the right words to express what I'm feeling. But after we've worked with movement, the words seem to flow easily from a place of centeredness.

VOICES FROM THE CIRCLE

I love to move. Movement is my natural language. When it comes to words, I feel so awkward and uncoordinated. I feel like I'm in alien territory.

Circledancing is one of the most moving experiences for me. In the dances, I feel our unity as a circle, and the larger way the circle embodies Spirit, and I also feel connected with generations of women over time and space.

I was deeply affected by the circle dance we did today. I often feel like I need more time than is given to learn new steps and process new information, so I was worried we were going to end too soon. But we stayed with it long enough for me to get the technical part down. I was really happy when we kept going. Then I started tuning into the energy and really enjoying myself. That was so healing!

civilization is not just a dream but an accomplished reality. While governments stockpile weapons and wage wars, musicians quietly get together to explore the frontiers of the creative spirit. Suicide bombings may dominate the headlines, yet for every suicide bomber, a thousand musicians are immersed in a sea of cross-cultural harmonies and rhythms. Flamenco music and Indian ragas, Australian didgeridoos and African drums—in the eyes and hearts of musicians, the whole world is a single, gloriously free playground. Without their gifts, our circles would not be the wild, magical, soul-stirring oases that they are.

> I lead a singing circle in a senior home. We meet every two weeks after dinner, and I teach beautiful chants and simple rounds. I don't talk about sacred geometry but I put a round table in the middle, with a cloth, and flowers, and a candle, and they get it. Sometimes I bring instruments. I started this circle a year ago and not only is it still going on, and people want it, but it keeps getting richer, and more and more satisfying. The participants are from their 60s into their 90s. Their memory is bad and I often have to remind them that the circle is happening. They come in their wheel chairs, with their walkers and crutches. It is just so beautiful to watch them as they get comfortable, close their eyes and pour their souls into the songs.

Music is like a powerful drug that enters our consciousness, whether we like it or not. So be selective in the music you listen to. If someone handed you a bottle of pills, you wouldn't just swallow them without making sure they were good for you. In the same way, you should pay close attention to the music you listen too. Don't pollute your energy field with the negative energy that bad music emits.

I would also encourage you to complain when music is played too loud, be it in stores, at clubs or concerts. We are currently witnessing a tragic epidemic in deafness. The proportion of second graders with some form of hearing loss has doubled in the past decade, while that of eighth graders has quadrupled. One out of five U.S. teens is suffering from noise induced hearing loss. To protect ourselves and future generations, we need to speak up.

Go Dancing!

◎ Go to a dance club.

◎ Go to a music and dance festival. There are festivals for lovers of jazz, reggae and world music, blues and country music. Whatever kind of music you enjoy, there's a festival just for you.

◎ If you're a young mother, look for some other young mothers who would like to get together and dance. Meet in someone's living room, put on some good music and let loose.

◎ In many communities, "barefoot boogies" have sprung up that are all about setting the body free. If your community doesn't yet have one, consider getting together with a few friends to start one. All you need is a big space and someone with good taste in music who is willing to be the disc jockey.

◎ Check out your local health club: Many offer classes that involve free-form creative movement.

◎ If freeform movement seems too scary, take a class in Tai Chi, or Yoga dance. Try contra dancing, or salsa dancing, or modern dance.

◎ Check out movement practices such as *Nia*, Gabrielle Roth's *Five Rhythms* work, *Continuum*, or *Authentic Movement*.

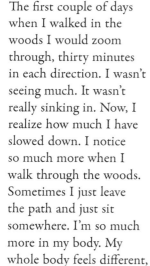

Resting

When we walk like (we are rushing), we print anxiety and sorrow on the earth. We have to walk in a way that we only print peace and serenity on the earth. . . . Be aware of the contact between your feet and the earth. Walk as if you are kissing the earth with your feet.

Thich Nhat Hanh

How well are we willing to care for our body? What would it mean to *really* respect it?

Whenever I ask this question, a common response I hear from women is that if they really respected their body, they would slow down and rest more. They would sleep for sixteen hours, like a cat, or hibernate for months like a bear.

Our addiction to incessant activity really *is* an addiction, and it's every bit as destructive as chain smoking or drinking. In our workaholic society, everything conspires to make us move faster, do more, and rest less.

But the greatest barrier to healthy living comes not from without but from within. That obstacle is, quite simply, the force of habit, which seeks to perpetuate itself. And so, we keep rushing and pushing, abusing our bodies and driving ourselves into the ground.

At one of my retreats, I led a guided meditation in which the women envisioned their life as a garden. Then, they picked up pen and paper and asked the garden to speak to them, as if it had a voice and a message to convey.

Afterwards, a woman called Elly read what she had written:

I'm your garden. You've tilled the soil, you've planted the seed. You can sit back now and relax. The flowers are growing, the fruits are blossoming. It's time to let it all be. Come and sink into me. Come sing and dance, swing in the fig trees, lay on the grass, soak up the sun, drink in the heady perfume of roses wet with dew. The gates are open; when are you going to come?

That all sounded very beautiful. But what did those poetic words mean to the everyday Elly who worked five long days a week, hated her job, and grappled with exhaustion and fibromyalgia? Curious, I initiated the following dialogue:

J: So! What does your everyday self say to that?

E: It says run like hell.

J: Run like hell?

E: Yeah.

J: Say more.

E: I'm terrified of being still. I've spent ten years trying to heal my childhood abuse, working on this garden, digging up all the weeds. I know hard work, but that's all I know. To just sink into who I am scares the shit out of me. I haven't been able to get past the wiring that the old childhood trauma created in me. Growing up, it was never safe to rest. That wiring is still a part of my physical body. I feel like I'm going to die if I hold still. There's a sense that to stay alive I have to keep moving.

J: So the fear says that if you stop moving, some kind of horror is going to overtake you?

E: Yes, and I'll die.

J: So your body doesn't know that it's in the garden.

E: No. My body wound tight as a cork screw. When I was doing yoga this morning I felt such pain through my ribs, as if I were wearing a corset.

Sheryl: Elly, I'm your friend. I've known you for a while now, and I can attest to the fact that you never stop. You're always

Voices from the Circle

I've had this pain in my shoulder all week. Yesterday, it was really shouting at me throughout our meditation. When I listened, I heard it telling me that I'm pushing too hard. All my life I've been pushing, pushing, pushing. I need to rest. Just acknowledging that out loud yesterday was so powerful. This morning I woke up for the first time without pain.

During our first training I was walking through the woods. I had just arrived and all the details of my life were still chasing me. And the words come into my mind: "I am moving at a speed where I can't be touched." That is still a major theme for me. Slowing down to the point that I can allow myself to be touched by life and by others.

It seems like a kind of patience is developing in me. I'm getting more aligned with nature's rhythms. I'm starting to understand that things happen and transform in their own time. I don't have to push.

This work is teaching me about tenderness and slowing down. About being gentle in every area of my life. The circle has made me less frenetic. I no longer match the crazy energy of the world around me. I listen to my own needs more and am better able to serve others. I feel a peace that moves with me throughout the day. I feel more in harmony with nature, because I am living in harmony with the rhythms of my own nature.

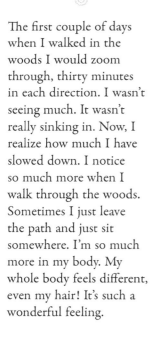

The first couple of days when I walked in the woods I would zoom through, thirty minutes in each direction. I wasn't seeing much. It wasn't really sinking in. Now, I realize how much I have slowed down. I notice so much more when I walk through the woods. Sometimes I just leave the path and just sit somewhere. I'm so much more in my body. My whole body feels different, even my hair! It's such a wonderful feeling.

going, always running. You never keep still. Your garden is inviting you to sit and not run.

J: If you were to stop running and rest in the garden, what would that look like?

E: It would mean slowing down. I'd curl up with a book. I'd stop worrying constantly about getting this and that done. I'd start playing music again. I'd spend more time at home. I'm scared though. I've never stopped moving. Never, ever.

J: Are you ready to try it?

E: I don't know. A part of me says yes, I am. I'm so exhausted. Another part of me says no.

J: Yes. That's fine. That's honest. While we're here, keep looking at this question. Thank you.

Elly is not alone; many of the women I work with are deeply fatigued. What they need is not just a good night's sleep or even a vacation, but a long, long rest. Yet even in their state of exhaustion, they often find it difficult to stop and do nothing at all.

If your intention is to align yourself with nature, then please remember that slowing down and resting are essential. In fact, I consider them among the most important spiritual disciplines we can practice. It may seem strange to call resting a discipline, but in the context of our speed-addicted society, it truly is. If we hope to live more gently, we need to take a good look at any habits that keep us locked into harsh, unhealthy patterns.

Fat and Beautiful

One of the great gifts of being part of a long-term women's circle is watching women discover their beauty. Every woman would like to feel beautiful, yet in our society, most don't—especially if they're fat.

In Circlework, physical appearance is not our focus. And yet, we find that as our self-love grows stronger, we become better able to love our body, as well. Our sense of physical beauty is, after all, inextricably interwoven with our sense of wholeness. When we don't love our body, it's never because of our physical flaws. We don't love our body because we don't love *ourselves*. How can we feel beautiful as long as we believe we're unworthy and unlovable? And this is, unfortunately, how all too many women feel about themselves.

Rebecca is a former lawyer in her fifties. For much of her life, she's hated her size. What made it worse was that she saw her own self-judgment reflected in the eyes of others.

"I feel like a fat person is everyone's worst nightmare," she says. "We're sort of a walking reminder of what they don't want to be. At least that's always been my feeling. Sometimes I have felt that I threaten people just by being."

Then, Rebecca started doing Circlework. In the circle, she found that women loved her for who she was. There was a deep sense of connection, comfort and safety that she had never experienced before. She felt no sense of judgment for having the body she had.

But there was one thing she noticed: Her clothing was very different from theirs. And so, she launched into a journey of self-discovery and transformation.

When I was an attorney, everything had to be impeccable and coordinated and professional, professional, professional. Professional earrings and shoes and the whole bit. I did that to a tee. But oh, it was so boring!

When I first came to Jalaja's circles, I had comfortable clothes. But some of the other women were wearing skirts and jewelry and sumptuous fabrics and these low cut, very feminine tops. In comparison, my clothes seemed sort of stark

VOICES FROM THE CIRCLE

Lying here, I felt filled with gratitude for my breath. I felt it touch every cell in my body, and I felt so deeply nourished by it. Is it my breath, our breath? It doesn't even belong to anyone, it just *is*. I experienced it as an expression of the incredible love that Spirit has for me. It was always there, but I never knew it. I couldn't recognize it because it didn't look the way I thought love should look. My eyes are opening and I am seeing things differently.

Circlework has given me many experiences of feeling accepted and validated in a much deeper, richer way than I've ever known in my life. It's amazing how much my body image has changed as a result. Now, when people tell me they love me and think I'm beautiful, I believe them. I've never been in this place before. It's not as if people never told me before that they loved me or that I was beautiful. They did, but Circlework has enabled me to take it in.

VOICES FROM THE CIRCLE

From the time I was a very tiny girl I thought I was ugly, fat, unacceptable, unlovable. My mother always told me I wasn't pretty. Now, I realize she thought that if I felt pretty, it would lead to sex, and that scared her. But back then, I believed her. I lived in a rural community, and when I got to first grade, I was a head taller than everyone else. They didn't have a desk to fit me, and they had to go to the fourth grade to find one. "Oh God, what's the matter with me?" I thought. Thank God for this circle! Thanks to you, I've discovered my beauty. The validation and support you gave me has healed a life-time of self-hatred.

◎

I loved going into my belly, it felt really good. I'm aware of having a big belly, of how big the space in there is. There's a part of me that really likes the spaciousness. I feel like there's room for a lot inside of me. But then my mind says, "Yeah, but don't keep breathing into it because it would be better if it were a little smaller . . ."

and utilitarian. I mean, I liked them fine, but suddenly they just seemed so Lutheran.

So I started with color. I said to myself, get a scarf. Get some color. You know, as a fat woman you're supposed to wear black and navy. No stripes and so on. But over time, I got more and more bold with color because it made me feel good. I thought, "I'm not doing that black and navy thing ever again. If it only comes in black and navy I'm not getting it." And I felt so much better.

The circle gave me permission. In the circle, it was okay that I was fat, so I realized I might as well be fat in red, instead of black, if red made me feel sexy. Or Mediterranean blue, or pink. I was inspired by some of these beautiful black women singers who are huge and wear these gorgeous gowns. They were my role models. And why not? Why should these little pinched-in people be my role models?

Then, I graduated to leggings, which was a big deal. Before, everything had to be loose. Nothing tight. But in the circle, we danced. If I was going to dance, I wanted something to move in. Plus, I needed to accept my legs, so I did the leggings thing.

I got to the point where I was wearing color, and leggings (though still paired with big baggy tops), and I even had some boas. My clothes were bright and playful, which was really important to me. But then, I started looking at some of the other women who brought in this really elegant femininity. It made me think, "Well, why don't you wear jewelry?" Skirts, too.

At some point, it became clear to me that all this baggy stuff was for the birds. I realized that even if I was heavy, I could wear things that were form fitting, and be attractive in them. That, too, was very liberating. "Oh, I guess I can have my neck show, and I can have boobs. Oh my god, I can be a woman. I can be feminine!" I stopped hiding. I became more present in my body, and less apologetic about it.

The women in the circle helped me find another vision for myself. For example, in the beginning I was wearing shoulder pads in everything, like my mom taught me. But at one retreat, someone asked, "Why do you wear shoulder pads?" I gave her the whole scoop about how making your shoulders look bigger would make your waist look smaller. And she just said, "You really think so? Take them out. Let's see the difference."

So I took one out and left one in, and I'm standing there and all these women are looking, and someone says, "I can't see a difference," and the next person says, "Yeah, I can't see a difference either."

So I started going without the shoulder pads, and the women still liked me. I know this really sounds ridiculous but that's how I felt about it—that they wouldn't like me without the extras.

There was never any kind of group pressure. I never got the sense that I was being judged. What the women were telling me was that they loved me. They were saying, "You're beautiful." With their own clothes, they were expressing that they felt beautiful, too. So that made me look at myself and ask, "What message am I giving myself through the clothes I wear?"

At one point, I was rooming with some other women who had this incredibly sexy underwear. I looked at my underwear and thought, "God, this stuff is so bad!" I said to myself, "Well, your mother always said this kind of underwear was comfortable, and when she was growing up, there were no alternatives. But now, you can get comfortable underwear that looks nice." So I bought myself new underwear. It's still not racy. It's still Midwestern, but I'm getting there in steps, and it feels nice, it feels really nice.

I've really absorbed the love and the acceptance that I

VOICES FROM THE CIRCLE

The meditation on being in my belly was hard. You know, I have a damn big one. I didn't want to be in touch with that. I have a cavernous belly which I regularly ignore. There is so much in there, so many memories and feelings. There's no way I could possibly touch all of that today. So I was aware of holding back. I was also aware that I was jealous of others who are thinner.

I participated in a week long circle. Most people sat on the floor, and I didn't really think that was good for me. There were a couple of other people sitting on chairs, but I was ashamed because I'm heavy. I thought they would say, "Look at the fat lady, she can't sit on the floor." So I forced myself to sit on the floor, until by the middle of the week I was in enormous pain. Then I said, "I can't do this anymore, and I started sitting on the couch." And I found it didn't seem to make any difference, nobody minded. They still liked me.

VOICES FROM THE CIRCLE

It's been so important to hear the women in my circle telling me they see me as beautiful, and to trust their sincerity. For the first time in my life I can hear and believe it, instead of focusing on my imperfections. I'm over fifty and my body is aging, and yet because of Circlework, I am happier with my body now than I was in my twenties and thirties.

received in the circle. It's become part of me. I have a sense that the circle is with me and behind me. That's a gift, a huge gift. Whenever I buy clothes, I think of the circle.

Today, I'm showing up more and hiding less. One of the reasons I love to wear bright colors and inappropriate clothing for a fat person was because I want to help liberate other fat people. I believe that anytime we come out of hiding, we help other people come out of hiding too. We liberate others when we liberate ourselves.

I'm going to shake my boobs when I dance, and people will just have to deal with it. Why should I live in a straitjacket?

Dressing the Goddess

In India, I witnessed how in the morning, priests would "wake up" the deities in the temple. They would wash and dress them with reverence, as if they were not mere statues but living, breathing beings.

This week, I invite you to experiment with doing the same for yourself. Pick a morning when you are not in a big rush, and see whether you could relate to your body and yourself as a goddess.

Many women habitually berate and belittle themselves. Instead, see what it feels like to speak gently and lovingly to yourself. When you wash your face or apply lotion, do so mindfully and with tenderness. Select clothes that celebrate who you are. Don't try to hide. Instead, affirm and emphasize your beauty.

Then, walk boldly and confidently into your day.

CHAPTER 14

A DIFFERENT KIND OF LEADERSHIP

One way to encapsulate the leadership required to create an alternative future is to consider the leader as primarily a convener— not leader as special person, but leader as a citizen, sometimes with legitimate power, willing to do those things that can initiate something new in the world. In this way, "leader" belongs right up there with cook, carpenter, artist, and landscape designer.[1]

Peter Block

In this chapter, I'd like to tell you a story about a woman who was called to lead a circle under challenging circumstances, and who in the process rediscovered the meaning of good leadership.

Samantha is a social worker as well as a graduate of the Circlework Training. A beautiful woman in her early forties, she has the pale face, clear gray eyes and blond curls of a Botticelli angel. She works for an agency that specializes in helping people cope with trauma. "Because of that," Samantha explains, "my job frequently takes me to communities that have witnessed a death or a crime and need help in dealing with the aftermath."

Recently, she had an experience that completely transformed her perception of what good leadership means. In our society, great leaders are usually portrayed as important people who take up a lot of space and tell other people what to do. Typically, they have larger-than-life personalities. Their presence is dazzling and charismatic and they possess special powers that enable them to save the day when nobody else can.

In Circlework, our image of good leadership is very different. Good circle leaders have no interest in being the center of attention. Instead, they listen, watch and pay close attention to what is happening. Like a mother who holds space in her womb for her baby to grow, good circle leaders give others space to be. Less intent on dispensing wisdom and guidance, their deepest desire is to help others access their *own* wisdom and guidance. Sure, they might initiate an activity or direct the process in a certain way. But their foremost commitment is to what is often called "holding the circle."

It's an apt term, because that's exactly what it feels like: Tenderly, we hold the circle in the bowl of our awareness. We listen very carefully—not only to what each participant says and does, but also to the unique soul of this particular circle. Where does it want to go? And since the soul always follows the scent of love, we might also ask, where is love trying to lead us? How can we, as leaders, contribute to making the circle a place where people can rediscover their true magnificence?

This was the kind of leadership Samantha had been learning about in our circles. But her agency had a very different understanding of the role and responsibilities of a leader. Her bosses had equipped her with detailed guidelines and protocols that she was expected to adhere to precisely. No matter what the situation was, there was always a clear agenda that she was supposed to implement.

For a long time, this structured, orderly approach to potentially chaotic situations had suited Samantha just fine. A self-confessed perfectionist, she liked feeling that she had everything under control, and that everything was neat, tidy and well- ordered.

"I'm a control freak," Samantha admits with a shrug. "But I'm changing. I'm starting to understand that when I get out of the way, miracles can happen."

In fact, recently a miracle *did* happen—at least that's what it felt like to her. It all started innocuously. As had happened so many times before, Samantha received an early morning call from her agency. Her supervisor gave her an address of what was apparently a home for developmentally disabled adults. Though she wasn't given any details, she knew that a resident had passed away. Based on what she'd been told, she assumed that the staff was in turmoil, and that her task would be to debrief them.

An hour later, Samantha pulled up in front of a dilapidated old building and knocked on the door. A disgruntled housekeeper let her in. It was at this point that Samantha realized just how wrong her assumptions had been. The staff, she learned, had basically fled. So instead of working with them, she was to work with the residents who, according to the housekeeper, had the mental capacity of five- or six-year-olds. The person who had died, a woman called Rose, had been their friend, and apparently, they were extremely upset about her death.

Stunned, Samantha sat down on the chair the housekeeper offered her. "Retarded" was the word that popped up in her mind. Politically incorrect, she knew, but there it was. This was a population she knew absolutely nothing about. How on earth was she supposed to deal with them? The very idea terrified her. Careful and conscientious, she hated being thrown into situations she felt ill prepared to handle.

Meanwhile, the housekeeper seemed totally oblivious to Samantha's distress. "Where the heck is everyone?" she scolded as she bustled around, trying to round up the residents.

Fifteen minutes later, she'd successfully herded them all into the large living room. There were about a dozen, somewhere between twenty and sixty-five years old. But as the housekeeper had said, they had the mindset of young children. Clearly unhappy and distressed, they flopped around, as restless as fish out of water.

"I didn't have a clue what to do," Samantha recalls. "I felt way out

VOICES FROM THE CIRCLE

I used to feel that when I was in charge, everything had to be pinned down and organized. Now I am learning to trust the circle. As a leader, I have learned that I don't have to have the answers, or be the focus of attention all the time. I can hold the space so others can contribute. I don't have to fill it.

of my league. But seeing as I was enrolled in the Circlework training, I decided to form a circle. I figured at least it couldn't do any harm."

Samantha had been given a detailed protocol on what to do with people who had unexpectedly lost a loved one. It had been designed with a very different population in mind, but since it was the only road map Samantha had, she decided she would follow it.

For starters, she was to give a talk about how sudden loss can affect people and what to expect in its aftermath. Bravely, Samantha launched into her talk, only to realize within short order that she might as well have been speaking Chinese. No one was paying her the slightest attention. The women were fidgety and obviously bored. Three men kept whispering to each other, becoming increasingly agitated until one of them started yelling, "I told you so, I told you so!"

"Please, folks, keep it down!" Samantha pleaded. And they did, for a few seconds. But soon, another crescendo of whispers escalated into a shouting match.

Frustrated, Samantha kept trying to discipline them. "Quiet, please!" she cried with a growing sense of irritation. "Calm down, everybody!"

And so they did. But no sooner had she resumed her talk than a woman interrupted her in mid-sentence.

"Miss," she said, "Are you married? That other lady who came to see us was married. Do you know her?"

Samantha felt uncomfortably like a school mistress with disciplinary problems.

"There are rules to this process," she declared, rather more sternly than she would have wished. They were not to interrupt.

But even as the words came out of her mouth, she knew it was hopeless—they didn't give a hoot about her rules. One woman had pulled off her socks and shoes and was inspecting her toes. Another was rocking back and forth, muttering to herself in an angry tone. Remembering the scene, Samantha shakes her head.

At this point, I was really starting to panic. I kept thinking, I have to do something, I have to do something! I *have* to get this situation under control.

But I couldn't figure out what to do. My mind was racing and so was my heart. There just didn't seem to be any way to move ahead according to plan.

Finally, I had to admit to myself: 'This just isn't working.'"

That's when I panicked for real. *Oh shit. I'm in deep trouble. That was my only thought. What the heck shall I do?*

It was amazing. The minute I asked that question, I heard a voice, as clearly as if someone were standing right next to me. I am not someone who hears voices. But in that moment, I swear I did.

"Just stop," it said. "Don't do anything. Just let go. Be quiet, open and receptive."

> *The most beautiful experience we can have is the mysterious. It is the fundamental emotion which stands at the cradle of true art and true science. Whoever does not know it and can no longer wonder, no longer marvel, is as good as dead, and his eyes are dimmed.*[2]
> Albert Einstein

What was this voice? Was it Samantha's unconscious, her soul, her spirit guide, her true self?

No matter what we call it, there's no question that we all carry within us a source of wisdom that's inaccessible to our conscious mind. Perhaps you too have experienced moments when thought ceased and some other source of guidance took over. Maybe a sudden revelation burst out of nowhere or an amazing insight appeared in a dream. Maybe a total stranger gave you some vital piece of information. Or perhaps you turned on the radio, and there was the answer you'd been looking for. We all have access to guidance. We might receive it in different ways, but if we're willing to stop and listen, it's available.

In hindsight, Samantha realized that up to this point, she'd been engaged in what I call "head-thinking." Head-thinking is the norm in our world, and what her agency had trained her to do. Head-thinkers love having step-by-step plans, set agendas, and clear objectives.

In the context of a society that is completely addicted to head-thinking and tends to dismiss heart-thinking as ineffectual, switching to heart-thinking can feel scary. It's even more so when we're holding a leadership position. Leaders, we've been taught, are supposed to keep everything under control. For a leader, losing control is a clear sign of failure.

Voices from the Circle

For many years, I believed I had nothing to give, so I was too scared to lead. This experience of leadership is new to me. It is changing my beliefs about myself. It feels great and so much more present and alive.

At least, that is the standard view. But in Circlework, we don't see it that way. Instead, we come to the circle with a clear intention of practicing heart-thinking. We don't have a set agenda or a predetermined structure. Instead, we try to listen to the circle's needs and follow its lead. Our desire is not so much to control the process as to be fully present with it. Instead of telling the circle where to go, we ask ourselves where *it* might want to go and how we might support that movement.

For leaders, this can be challenging because it means we have to let go of the comforting illusion that we know what's about to happen. In reality, we rarely do, nor does our heart have a problem with this. But for the mind, such uncertainty feels alarming. This is especially true if, like Samantha, we've been taught that our job is to keep everything under control, and that head-thinking is the key to doing that. Terrible things will happen, so we've been led to believe, if we dare to topple the dictatorship of their mind.

If you're involved in some form of group leadership and you like to have a plan, then by all means, go for it. Make a plan, if you want—or two, or three. Prepare in whatever way gives you a feeling of confidence. After all, the more relaxed you are, the better. Just be prepared to let your plans go at the drop of a hat. Hold them with a light touch, leaving space for miracles and delightful surprises. Don't cling to a rigid agenda that would squelch the magic of the circle.

The Ritual Unfolds

Magic was, indeed, what Samantha and her new friends experienced, once she let go of her agenda and allowed her heart to open.

Until that point, she'd been trying valiantly to stick with her protocol. Caught up in head-thinking, she'd split the group into two camps: she and her agency on one side, the residents on the other. Unwittingly, she had fallen into "us-versus-them" thinking, which lies at the root of all warfare. As a result, she felt very separate from the residents, and they from her. Unable to hear, accept, or contain their emotions, she was more intent on controlling than serving them. Yet the harder she tried, the more they resisted. And so, what was intended to be a healing environment became a battleground. Instead of helping them find inner peace, she was waging war on them.

Fortunately, years of Circlework practice had prepared Samantha how to do exactly what her guidance was recommending: Stop, and listen. Taking a deep breath, she shifted from her head to her heart. Then, she allowed herself to drop into a state of quiet, receptive presence. She gave up all pretense to being the kind of leader her agency had trained her to be, and instead gave herself permission to listen deeply, both within and without. Thus, in the midst of a crisis, she made the leap from control-based to heart-centered leadership.

"What happened next," she tells me, "taught me in an unforgettable way how our own consciousness affects that of others.

> It was amazing, truly. You see, the minute I gave up my agenda, and became totally present and receptive, the residents sensed my openness. And suddenly, they started to sob. A minute ago, they'd been yelling and creating total chaos. Now, they were totally focused and present. It was as if we had walked from a battlefield into a beautiful sanctuary. Really, it blew my mind. I could not believe what was happening.

Samantha was fortunate—these men and women had not only

the intellectual capacity of young children, but also their total authenticity. They weren't interested in hiding their feelings or in pleasing anyone. Like clear mirrors, they showed Samantha exactly how she was affecting them. As long as she kept trying to keep them under control, nothing worked. But once she let go, and became receptive, they too shifted.

VOICES FROM THE CIRCLE

Circlework has reconnected me with an inner source of wisdom and knowing that had been blocked for so long. It has helped me tap into a huge well of insight and creativity and has opened me up to a much broader vision of myself.

And with that, the whole battle came to an end. Her heart, she realized, had no interest in controlling them. All it wanted was to simply *be* with them and offer them her compassion. Instead of labeling them "different" or "abnormal," she began to notice how special and unique they all were. Resting in a pool of inner stillness and peace, she actually began to enjoy their company.

Samantha had brought crayons and paper, and after a while, she started writing down what the residents were saying. "Rose was beautiful. We loved Rose so much. Rose had beautiful eyes." They were simple statements, yet imbued with deep emotion and a profound sense of caring. Samantha helped her new friends compile a long list of everything they'd said, written in large multi-colored letters. Once they decided it was done, they hung it up on the wall.

"It felt like the perfect ritual," Samantha tells me with a smile. "And yet it wasn't planned; it evolved naturally once I stopped trying to 'do' anything and just listened. The sense of separation between us had dissolved completely. I was no longer seeing them as 'retarded people' and they were no longer seeing me as an authority figure. We'd become friends who were sharing our sorrow."

Samantha left the residence feeling great. But later that evening, she started second-guessing herself. After all, her responses had been light years removed from how she was *supposed* to respond according to agency rules. In the moment, everything had felt so right, but was it really? The housekeeper had told her that the previous night, the residents had acted out their frustration and stress. Some had nightmares. Others had gotten into a fight and broke some windows.

"What's going to happen tonight?" Samantha worried.

But the next day, a staff member called and said, "Thank you! I don't know what you did, but they were so different after you left. They had a completely peaceful night. Nobody acted out at all."

Samantha sighed with relief.

"This experience has been pivotal for me," she tells me with a smile. "Letting go of my agenda and simply listening was what made an unworkable situation workable. I've gained a whole new appreciation for the power of *not* doing, not fixing, not trying to control things. For me, this is what true leadership looks and feels like. It's authentic, it's powerful and it's healing. And I'm proud of myself for having had the courage to model that kind of leadership."

I was proud of Samantha too, for I felt that she was now embodying the kind of leadership that the Circlework Training is designed to nurture—leadership that is authentic, receptive, healing and imbued with the spirit of service.

We're All Leaders

Everyone is, at times, a leader, be it within their family, at work, or in their community. Often, we approach leadership, much as Samantha did, with set ideas about what it should look like and what results it should achieve. Yet as Samantha discovered, the best leader is the best follower.

Next time you're in a leadership role, try to remember her story and see whether you, too, could let go of your agenda. Instead, just listen, try to understand the other's needs and let Spirit use you as an instrument of healing and empowerment.

CHAPTER 15

Ripples of Change: Circlework and Activism

The truest and deepest joy comes not only from recognizing one's essential nature as joy, but in expressing that joy in wise, focused, radical action which implements justice, harmony, balance, and compassion. The joy of which we are speaking is not a private, narcissistic joy; it is a joy that reflects the essential nature of reality and also the deepest meaning of human life as revealed by all the great prophets and mystics of humanity—a meaning that can only be discovered in radical, selfless service and the commitment to a life dedicated to living joy in sacred relationship with all beings. 1

Andrew Harvey & Carolyn Baker

When Mia came to the Circlework Training, she was primarily looking to heal *herself*. But what she experienced in the circle made her think anew about her work as an activist.

Most of her activist friends were fighters. They were tough, strong, passionate and dedicated, but also somewhat cynical. They tended to be head- rather than heart-thinkers. Mia started to wonder, was there another way? Could activism be an act of beauty, kindness, magic and feminine power? Could it reflect the values she'd been cultivating in our circles?

She decided to give it a try. The focus would be the anniversary of a tragedy that had occurred in her community some years ago. Here's her story:

There was this guy in my community, a student at the local engineering school, who hated women. And on December 6, 1989, he shot and killed thirteen women before killing himself. Ever since, we've held an annual gathering to commemorate that massacre.

I talked it over with my friends, and we decided we wanted to use that anniversary to highlight the ongoing problem of violence against women. But we wanted to do it in a new way that would invoke the healing power of the circle. We wanted it to be a positive experience for us, and for everyone involved.

December 6th turned out to be a really cold winter night. Nonetheless, over a hundred participants showed up at the meeting place. We explained our plan and gave each one of them their assignment. Then, we all went to this busy intersection in the middle of town.

There, we formed three concentric circles, with different activities going on in each one. Some roles were reserved for women, other for men. In one circle, for example, women were holding signs with statistics about violence against women. In the center, a woman played a sad but beautiful violin while around her, other women moved and danced, sometimes abruptly dropping to the ground as if shot. There was no talking whatsoever, everything unfolded in total silence, except for the violin.

This turned out to be the most sacred and amazing action I have ever been involved in. Not only was it healing and cathartic, but it was also extremely successful, in the sense that we received a lot of media attention.

VOICES FROM THE CIRCLE

Every day I pray for everyone in my circle. I feel a part of that circle daily; in the midst of my life I feel their presence. It has made it easier to carve out time for the kind of prayer and meditation I need to do regularly to stay centered and balanced. I no longer allow myself to get too busy. There's a sense of responsibility to the circle to take myself seriously and make the time I need to stay centered. There's a greater sense of peace and more spaciousness in my life.

We had booked a coffee house so that after the event, we'd have a place to debrief. It was packed, and so many women came up to me, very emotional, to tell me how healing this event had been for them and how safe they had felt.

Terrible things happen, and there is rarely a place to honor and grieve it. That night, the circle helped us create that space. It was so hopeful . . . we were all so infused with hope, for each other and for the future. It still warms me to think about it.

And it changed me as an activist. I see now how the softness that is essential to Circlework holds such potential for planetary healing. I feel like we called on the circle, we had faith in it. And in return, it graced us with such a powerful healing experience.

Why Every Activist Needs a Circle

If it were up to me, every activist would have a circle. Of course, many already *do*. But what I'm talking about now is not a work circle, but a different kind of circle: one that is exclusively dedicated to self-healing and nourishment.

Burnout is a huge problem—for all of us, but especially for activists, who often grapple with evils that most people prefer to turn a blind eye to. Overworked and underpaid, they're keenly aware of the suffering that surrounds them, and of the dangers that threaten our world. And yet, they refuse to take refuge in numbness and denial.

Such people are heroes, in my eyes. But heroes are human, too. Having worked with many activists, I've have seen how deeply exhausted they get, sometimes to the point of physical collapse.

Part of the problem, I've come to understand, are guilt and fear. Many activists love Mother Earth so deeply, and are so keenly aware of the threats to her well-being, that they feel they must do everything in their power to save her. But there are limits to what we as individuals can accomplish. Once we've made our contribution, we must be willing to let go. For many activists, this is hard. No matter how much they do, it never feels like it's enough.

Most activists place a high value on service. They recognize that the "me, me, me" attitude of consumer culture is unsustainable, and that greed and violence are antithetical to the laws of nature. Yet this very passion for service can make it difficult for them to take good care of *themselves*. In theory, they understand that nobody benefits if they get sick and tired. They realize their burnout would be a loss to everyone. Yet in practice, they often find it extremely difficult to stop.

If you are an activist, I would remind you that you, too, are the product of a society that is addicted to constant thinking and doing. Most of us are, to some extent, affected by this addiction. Be willing to make an honest assessment: "Am I using my service to the world as an excuse to avoid bringing my mind and body to a full stop? Am I forcing my body to bear the brunt of my addiction to thinking and doing?"

So much in our environment is designed to make us feel that we aren't enough, that we have to be more and have more and do more. Activists are particularly vulnerable to this mental trap because the stakes are so high. "When I think of my grandbabies," my friend Rosie tells me, "I can't sleep at night. I know I'm driving myself too hard. But how can I rest, knowing what's at stake?"

Stopping is scary, because to stop is to relinquish any illusion of having things under control. Are we willing to let go? Are we willing to face our fears without jumping into action? Can we simply sit with them and hold them in compassion? Are we willing to face the possibility that we may *not* succeed in saving our world?

It helps to have a circle where together, we can look at whatever comes up. In my experience, there is nothing so heavy or dark that the circle cannot hold it. Individually, what we're up against can feel overwhelming. But together, we can lay it gently

Voices from the Circle

Doing Circlework completely changed the way I viewed my family. Previously, I never used to think of us as a circle. Now, I do. Luckily for me, my husband is on the same page. Now, we make sure that each child has a voice. We make sure they have their own time to speak and we really acknowledge their role in the family. The kids feel included in everything—they feel this sense of communion. It used to be so different. Basically, my husband and I used to be the bus drivers and everyone else was along for the ride. Now, we're a community. When the weekend comes, they'd rather spend time with us than with their friends. So all their friends come over to our house, which is wonderful.

into the bowl of our mandala. We can grieve for it, talk about it, pray over it. Beginning within, we can transform darkness into light.

On our own, this can be very difficult to do. Remember Ron's grief over the AIDS-related deaths of his friends? Ron was very clear in his assessment: Alone, he could never have allowed his emotions to surface and be transformed. Sure, there are times when we can heal our wounds on our own. Yet, especially in times of intense collective turbulence, having a circle can be incredibly helpful and potentially life-saving.

We all need places where we don't have to be strong or brave, where we can wail out our grief, roar with rage and tremble with fear. This holds true for all of us, but especially for activists, healers and world-changers. We need places where we can voice our fatigue, and be lovingly encouraged to confront any self-abusive habits that might be weakening us. We need sanctuaries where we can lay our burdens down, reveal our brokenness, and be loved back to wholeness.

A Different Understanding of Activism

The circle is one of nature's most ancient organizational tools. For billions of years, it's been organizing clouds of cosmic gasses, galaxies and planets, suns and moons, spider webs and birds' nests. For activists, too, circles are an essential tool. Whether our goal is to create a community center, save a forest, or defend social rights, the circle can help us join forces more effectively. It can bond us in strong, durable ways, but it's also flexible enough to adapt to the wide-ranging needs of our diverse communities.

Another great benefit of circles is that they require absolutely no technology. Today, a large part of the human population still has no access to running water or electricity. Yet *everyone* has access to the circle. A truly democratic tool, it completely levels the playing field between rich and poor. Whether we gather in a mansion or in a dusty village square, either way, we

VOICES FROM THE CIRCLE

Circlework is not about going to the circle on Saturdays, it's about taking it home. It's about how we live from day to day, what we do in our lives and in our communities. By making this commitment to the circle I have committed to be conscious in all areas of my life.

can use circles to invoke the spirit of peace, healing and unity.

As I see it, spirituality and activism are twins. Spirituality leads to the realization that we are one—one human family, one world, one cosmos. Once we realize this, we cannot condone injustice and violence or turn a blind eye on the suffering of others. So from spiritual awakening, a straight line leads to compassionate action.

Psychological work, too, is an essential strand of this braid. We all carry within ourselves the seeds of the very darkness that we are trying to defeat in the world. If we fail to become conscious, we may unwittingly worsen the very problems we are seeking to overcome. Tending to our inner world is therefore one form of activism, tending to the outer world another. Both are necessary, and neither can bear fruit without the other.

But what exactly do we mean by "activism?" According to Wikipedia, "Activism consists of efforts to promote, impede, or direct social, political, economic, or environmental reform or stasis with the desire to make improvements in society." Another dictionary defines it as "the policy or action of using vigorous campaigning to bring about political or social change."

Vigorous campaigning, however, is not everyone's cup of tea. What if we want to contribute to social change, yet aren't comfortable with the standard pathways for doing so? Might there be another, more inclusive understanding of activism?

I believe there is. When we speak of activism, we usually think of organized activities. Yet beyond that, we all have opportunities to act in ways that reflect our desire for social justice and peace. Whether or not we're "official" activists, we're always taking action, all the time. Every day, we're making choices that will impact not only our own future but also that of others.

When I first created Circlework, I didn't view it as a form of activism. Today, I do, because I've seen the impact that circles can have, not only on our own lives but on the lives of those around us. Every circle

VOICES FROM THE CIRCLE

The day that I learned that my youngest daughter, who is an alcoholic, had relapsed and put my grandson in danger, I was in such pain. My heart felt so utterly broken, I could barely breathe. I literally stumbled to the computer to put out a cry for help to my circle sisters. And within ten minutes, several had called me and one was on my doorstep. I felt so supported, by her and by my whole circle. There were arms holding me in ways I had never experienced before.

is like a little pebble that gets tossed into a still lake. Long after the pebble comes to rest at the bottom, ripples keep spreading across the surface. A greater sense of well-being and ease arises. A long stagnant relationship bursts into bloom. And above all, the way we relate to ourselves and others changes. Without explicitly trying to inspire compassionate action, Circlework does so very naturally.

I think, for example, of a group of Jewish and Arab women I worked with in Northern Israel, near the Lebanese border. In the circle, they came to know and love each other. Prejudice and distrust gave way to caring and respect.

Then, in 2006, war erupted between Israel and Lebanon. Within Israel, relations between Jews and Arabs became more strained than ever. Yet the women who'd participated in my circles did not buy into the general uptick in Jewish-Arab hostility. Now, more than ever, they were there for each other. One might call another to say, "Don't take that road. It's not safe right now. Go the long way round." They'd pass on warnings about check points and make sure everyone was okay. They didn't care whether the woman on the other end of the line was Jewish or Arab. They just wanted her to be safe.

These women were not engaging in activism in the usual sense of the word. They were simply acting in accordance with the authentic desire of their hearts and souls. The circle had caused a shift in their attitude that was now rippling out into the world.

Closer to home, the effects of Circlework are similar. When Sophia, a mother in her forties, joined a two-year Circlework Training, she could never have foreseen the ripples this would create, first in her inner world, and then in her entire community.

Sophia used to think of certain people as kin, others as strangers. Yet in the circle, she bonded deeply and intimately with women whom she would ordinarily have felt no sense of kinship with. Her sense of separation crumbled, and she realized that all women were her sisters, no matter how different their backgrounds or circumstances might be.

VOICES FROM THE CIRCLE

The distinction I used to feel between our time in the circle and outside of the circle has dissolved. It's happening all the time. It's become my way of being in the world. What we do here is what I am committed to doing in the world.

Soon after Sophia's circle ended, she read a disturbing article in her local paper about a women's shelter that was in danger of closing because of funding cuts.

In the article, it said, "This women's shelter serves the following counties . . ." I read the list and saw that my county was listed there too. In fact, it said that a huge number of the women who come for help are from my hometown.

Women's shelter? I didn't even know we had a women's shelter, or that we needed one. I had no idea. I didn't realize there were women in our town who were getting battered and raped and who needed immediate help and shelter. We live in a really small town and we don't have any homeless people, so it's not visible. But it's there, way more than I ever realized.

Thanks to her experience with Circlework, Sophia responded very differently to this information than she formerly would have. Not only did she feel an immediate and undeniable sense of solidarity with the women served by this shelter, but she also felt responsible, in the true sense of the word—able to respond.

All of a sudden I was aware of these women whom I hadn't been aware of before. I felt like I had some sisters who needed help. And I thought, "Oh my God. Somebody should do something!"

And then . . . "Well, no, *I* should do something." It was a direct result of being in circle and relating to women who are very different from me. Because of Circlework, I felt like this was my community too. My awareness had expanded.

You know all the extra stuff that every American household has? Instead of just giving it to the resale shop in town like everyone else does, I started organizing to take it to the women's shelter and doing little fundraising things for them.

Suddenly I had people calling and emailing me whom I had never met. They would say, "Oh, I heard you are collecting things for the women's shelter. What else do they need? I have a television, I have computers, can you come by and pick them up?"

So this little connection I made opened up the awareness of all these other people. I felt so much more connected with my community because of this.

I started raising people's awareness about this shelter. I explained that there were a lot of people in our community whom we never saw but who needed help. I started driving back and forth to the shelter with carloads of baby clothes and other things. And after talking to people about how this shelter had lost its funding, some friends of mine decided to get together and do a fundraiser, and we raised $11,000 in one night.

See, it was a direct carry-over from Circlework. When I found out that there were these women in trouble who needed help, I felt like it could easily have been me. There wasn't a big gap between them and me. I knew that by helping them I was helping myself, and my daughter, and my mother.

Sophia wasn't driven by a sense of guilt or by a "should." Because her actions reflected the spontaneous response of an open heart, she felt inspired rather than depleted by her work for the shelter. "That microcosm macrocosm thing" she refers to is, of course, the awareness of our interconnectedness that is so basic to the practice of Circlework, and that very naturally inspires a sense of caring and compassion.

Guidance Is Internal

Recently I reviewed the footage of those electrifying seconds in 1969 when the Apollo space shuttle lifted off towards the moon. I'd watched it before, but had never noticed the wording of the countdown. It starts predictably:

"Sixty seconds to take-off . . . fifty seconds . . . forty seconds . . . eighteen, seventeen . . ."

But at this point, the countdown is suddenly interrupted by the startling words, "GUIDANCE IS INTERNAL!"

Then, it continues, "Fifteen, fourteen, thirteen . . ." And so, the great bird lifts off into the heavens, ushering in a new era of exploration that would have been unthinkable a mere century ago.

You and I may never fly to the moon. Still, we too are on a journey into new and uncharted terrain. In this day and age, we can no longer rely on the old authorities upon whose guidance we once depended. To survive this adventure, we'll need to look within for guidance.

This is new. For most of human history, spiritual power always resided in the hands of religious authority figures who told us what to believe and what to do. No matter what happened, we trusted in the advice of priests, shamans, and other spiritual power brokers.

Now and then, a rebel would come along who questioned those authorities. Take, for example, the man who later came to be known as Gautama Buddha, the awakened one. For years, he practiced austerities that would, so his elders assured him, surely lead to enlightenment. But they didn't. No matter how much he fasted and deprived himself, the state of inner peace and freedom he sought eluded him.

One day, so the story goes, he was sitting under a tree when a village woman passed by. Seeing his emaciated form, she offered him a bowl of creamy milk rice. And instead of rejecting it, as he formerly would have, he accepted it, and ate.

Eating a bowl of milk rice might seem like a small thing. But for the Buddha, it was a act of revolution. As a monk, he was supposed to avoid women and everything associated with the feminine. Yet in this moment, he accepted both the nurturing care of a woman and the milk of a cow, who in India is identified with Mother Earth. And so, in that simple act, he was abandoning the safe confines of established religion forever. Instead of trying to transcend the world, he would henceforth honor and embrace it.

VOICES FROM THE CIRCLE

Circlework is effecting a real and lasting shift in my life. This is not just a momentary realization from which I'll wake up tomorrow and find it's gone.

This was the last meal the Buddha ate before his enlightenment: Finally, the portal to freedom appeared. Later, asked to prove his realization, he would touch Mother Earth, calling upon her as his witness: He had come home—to her, and to himself.

The Buddha was a radical, in the original sense of the word, which means "of the root." He wanted to know the root of love, of life, of suffering—not from hearsay but from personal experience. Years later, lying on his death bed, his last words were: "Be a light unto yourself."

Today, more and more people are following his advice. While they might listen to spiritual teachers, they reserve the right to make their own choices. They are less eager to follow rules and more prone to questioning them.

This is by no means an easy path to walk. Sometimes, the voice of our own guidance is obscured by layers of mental business or emotional turbulence. Sometimes, we're simply lazy: It's much easier to simply rely on the guidance of outer authority figures than to patiently seek out our own truth.

Voices from the Circle

Circlework enables me to be the change I want to see in the world, as opposed to just demonstrating against what I *don't* like.

Having a circle can be a big help. Since time immemorial, our ancestors used circle gatherings to create portals through which guidance could enter. Of course, guidance is a mysterious thing, and not under our control. On the other hand, it's not nearly as hard to access as we're often led to believe. Everything hinges on our willingness to turn within, listen, and open our own deepest truth. Whether we're artists or activists, educators or business people, this inner alignment is crucial to our success. Without it, our actions will remain ineffectual, no matter how hard we try to make a difference.

Circlework doesn't tell us what to do. It isn't a place we go to receive advice. Instead, it invites us to listen deeply to ourselves. Also, it helps us calm our mind, making us more receptive to the guidance we need. In this way, it helps us realize the truth of those three simple words: *Guidance is internal.*

Often, the guidance women receive in the circle concerns their inner world. But I've also seen them come away with specific instructions for taking action in the outer world. Some go home to start new careers and relationships. Others quit their jobs or file for divorce. Sometimes the changes initiated in the circle are pleasant, other times they're painful. Either way, insofar as they reflect a woman's alignment with her deepest truth, they are necessary and ultimately healing.

Twice, circle participants have received clear visions of retreat centers that wanted to be created. Both have successfully realized their dreams, and the sanctuaries they built—one near Victoria, Canada, the other in the Palestinian city of Bethlehem—are thriving to this day, and are serving as places of refuge and healing to many.

Circles as Immune Cells

I sometimes compare our circles to immune cells. The human family, as a whole, is suffering; our consciousness is disjointed and unhealthy. Yet in our circles, we gain access to a consciousness is centered, clear and wise. Together, we drink from a bowl of medicine that can restore our collective health. In such moments, our circle transforms into an immune cell.

A single immune cell might seem to be a tiny thing, puny and powerless. But then, immune cells don't function in isolation. When they appear, they appear in the thousands or millions. The same is true of circles: Our power lies in our numbers. As Jean Bolen writes in *The Millionth Circle*, the power of circles to change our world grows exponentially as their numbers increase. Even a single circle can help its members keep their balance amidst the world's insanity. But multiply that times a thousand, and you're looking at an immense—and so-far largely untapped—force for planetary healing.

Imagine thousands, tens of thousands of circles, all committed to peace and to the empowerment of the feminine. Clearly, we have at our disposal an immense—and as yet largely untapped—force for planetary healing. Might we, instead of building more weapons of

VOICES FROM THE CIRCLE

Doing a long circle is like waking up. I can't live like I used to. I realize that my inner state of consciousness matters so much more than I knew. Circlework is teaching me to stay awake. It's just too challenging unless you are awake.

mass destruction, start building weapons of mass healing? For that is, in essence, what our circles are.

As we open in stillness and receptivity, we find that we are not only being healed, but also prepared to take authentic action. From here, we can move forward with confidence. Instead being driven by fear, and by a false belief that it's up to us to save the world, we feel inspired by trust in the goodness of life, and by a clear awareness of our own calling. Connected in love, centered in truth, we realize we are fully capable of facing the unknown with clear eyes and a peaceful, courageous heart.

Noticing the Ripples

I invite you to make a commitment that for the next 24 hours you'll pay close attention to all the ripples you send out into the world.

For example, every time you make a financial transaction, whether you're buying potatoes at your local farmers market or ordering something online, take a moment to consider all the people who will be affected. In your mind's eye, trace the imaginary path of that money through time and space.

Notice what you put into the trash. Notice the quality of your voice. Notice how the many small choices you make all send out ripples into your environment.

Every time you talk with someone, or communicate via text or email, try to be aware of the energy you are emitting. Sometimes our impact on others is healing, sometimes it's toxic. Don't judge yourself, just notice.

Now What?

Our journey into the magic of Circlework is drawing to a close. Or perhaps, it's just beginning? It all depends on you. Hopefully, this book has given you a clear sense of the healing and peace, inspiration and empowerment that Circlework can facilitate. I hope, also, that it has deepened your sense of connection to the circle as an inner source of wisdom, guidance and spiritual sustenance.

If you would like to go deeper into the magic of Circlework, here are a few suggestions:

◎ Go to *www.magicofcirclework.org* and enter "circlemagic" as your temporary password to enjoy the free bonus materials included with your purchase of this book, including audio recordings, videos, recommended music and more.

◎ Form a reading group. Every week, read one or two chapters and discuss them.

◎ Think about how you might bring some of the principles of Circlework to groups and circles you're already involved with.

◎ Come to the Circlework Training and learn to lead circles in your own community. Scholarships may be available for applicants who cannot afford the training fees.

◎ To learn more about the "how-to" aspects of Circlework,

consider purchasing the *Circlework Training Manual.* Published by the Institute for Circlework, you can order it at *www. magicofcirclework.org.*

I'm always happy to hear from you. You can connect with me at *www.jalajabonheim.com* or on Facebook at *https://www.facebook. com/sacredego.*

Thank you, and may the circle bless you with wholeness, peace and balance.

Included in your purchase of *The Magic of Circlework* are free bonus materials, including recommended music, helpful links, and much more. Please go to **www.magicofcirclework.com** to access the bonus materials. Here, you can also purchase the Circlework Training Manual. Your temporary password is: **circlemagic.**

ENDNOTES

INTRODUCTION

1. Vivek Murthy, Work and the Loneliness Epidemic, *Harvard Business Review*, October 2017.

CHAPTER 1

1. Yaya Diallo and Mitchell Hall, *The Healing Drum: African Wisdom Teachings,* Rochester, VT, Destiny Books 1989, p. 58.

2. "Small is Beautiful" in *The Radical Humanist,* Vol. 37, No. 5 (August 1973), p. 22.

3. From *The Essential Rumi,* Translations by Coleman Barks with John Moyne, HarperSanFrancisco 1995, p. 137, reprinted by permission.

CHAPTER 2

1. Parker Palmer, *A Hidden Wholeness: The Journey Toward an Undivided Life*, San Francisco: Jossey Bass, 2004, p. 59.

CHAPTER 3

1. John G. Neihardt, *Black Elk Speaks: Being the Life Story of a Holy Man of the Oglala Sioux,* University of Nebraska Press, Lincoln, NE, 1961, p 198.

2. Thich Nhat Hanh & Rachel Neumann, *Calming the Fearful Mind: A Zen Response to Terrorism,* Parallax Press 2001.

3. Peter Miller, "The Genius of Swarms," *National Geographic Magazine,* July 2007.

4. Lynne McTaggart, *The Intention Experiment: Using Your Thoughts to Change Your Life and the World,* Free Press, 2007.

5. Quoted in Corbett, Sara, "Carl Jung and the Holy Grail of the Unconscious," *New York Times,* September 16, 2009, MM 34.

CHAPTER 4

1. From *Women in Praise of the Sacred,* edited by Jan Hirshfield, HarperCollins, 1994, reprinted by permission.

2. From *I Heard God Laughing: Poems of Hope and Joy,* Renderings of Hafiz by Daniel Ladinsky, Penguin Books 1996, 2006, used by permission.

CHAPTER 7

1. Round Dance of the Cross," in Acts of John 94.1–4. Translation by Barbara E. Bowe in "Dancing into the Divine: The Hymn of the Dance in the Acts of John," *Journal of Early Christian Studies* 7:1 (1999), 83–104.

CHAPTER 9

1. Hildegard of Bingen, *Devotions, Prayers & Living Wisdom,* edited by Mirabai Starr, Sounds True, 2008, p. 41.

CHAPTER 12

1. Francis Weller, *The Wild Edge of Sorrow,* North Atlantic Books, 2015, p. 104-105

CHAPTER 14

1. Peter Block, "Leading is Convening," *Perdido* 15, no. 2, 2008.
2. Albert Einstein in *Living Philosophies*, Simon and Schuster, New York 1931.

CHAPTER 15

1. Andrew Harvey & Carolyn Baker, *Return to Joy,* IUniverse 2016, p. 56.

Resources

Anderson, Sherry, and Patricia Hopkins (Contributor). *The Feminine Face of God: The Unfolding of the Sacred in Women.* New York: Bantam, 1992.

Baldwin, Christina. *Calling the Circle: The Firsts and Future Culture.* New York: Bantam, 1998.

Baldwin, Christina and Ann Linnea. *The Circle Way: A Leader in Every Chair.* San Francisco: Berrett-Koehler Publishers, 2010.

Bolen, Jean Shinoda. T*he Millionth Circle: How to Change Ourselves and the World.* Boston: Conari Press,1999.

Bolen, Jean Shinoda. *Moving Toward the Millionth Circle.* San Francisco: Conari Press, 2013. (*Note:* LK selection added)

Boyes-Watson, Carolyn. *Peacemaking Circles and Urban Youth: Bringing Justice Home.* St. Paul, MN: Living Justice Press, 2008. (*Note:* LK selection added)

Cahill, Sedonia. *The Ceremonial Circle.* New York: HarperCollins, 1992.

Carnes, Robin Deen and Sally Craig. *Sacred Circles: A Guide to Creating Your Own Women's Spirituality Group.* San Francisco: HarperCollins, 1998.

Duerk, Judith. *Circle of Stones: Woman's Journey to Herself.* San Francisco: New World Library, 2004. (*Note:* LK selection added)

Engel, Beverly. *Women Circling The Earth: A Guide to Fostering Community, Healing and Empowerment.* Deerfield Beach, FL: Health Communications, 2000.

Fitzgerald, Maureen F., PhD. *A Woman's Circle: Create a Peer Mentoring Group for Advice, Support, Networking and Connection.* CenterPoint Media, 2016.

Garfield, Charles. *Wisdom Circles: A Guide to Self-discovery and Community Building in Small Circles.* New York: Hyperion, 1999.

Kauth, Bill. *A Circle of Men: The Original Manual for Men's Support Groups.* New York: St. Martin's Press, 2015.

Kauth, Bill and Zoe Alowan. *We Need Each Other: Building Gift Community.* Ashland, OR: Silver Light Publications, 2011. (*Note:* LK selections added)

Macy, Joanna and Molly Brown. *Coming Back to Life: The Updated Guide to the Work that Reconnects*. Canada: New Society Publishers, 2014.

Marks, Kate. *Circle of Song: Songs, Chants, and Dances for Ritual Celebration*. Full Circle Press; revised edition 1994.

Mihaltses, Melusine. *Gathering for Goddess: A Complete Manual for Priestessing Women's Circles*. Schertz, TX: Feminine Divine Works, 2012.

Mihaltses, Melusine. *Living Goddess Spirituality: A Feminine Divine Priestessing Handbook*. Schertz, TX: Feminine Divine Works, 2012 (*Note:* LK selection added).

Moses, Christine. *The Wisdom of Circles: Gathering Women for Conscious Community*. CreateSpace Independent Publishing, 2016.

Neal, Craig and Patricia Neal. *The Art of Convening: Authentic Engagement in Meetings, Gatherings, and Conversation*. San Francisco: Berrett-Koehler Publishers, 2011.

Palmer, Parker. *A Hidden Wholeness: The Journey Toward an Undivided Life*. San Franciso: Jossey-Bass, 2009.

Pranis, Kay. *The Little Book of Circle Processes: A New/Old Approach to Peacemaking*. Intercourse, PA: Good Books, 2005.

Pranis, Kay, Barry Stuart and Mark Wedge. *Peacemaking Circles: From Crime to Community*. St. Paul, MN: Living Justice Press, 2003.

Preston-Pile, Cindy and Irene Woodword. *Traveling with the Turtle: A Small Group Process in Women's Spirituality and Peacemaking*. Corvallis, OR: Pace e Bene Press, 2006.

Rosenberg, Marshall. *Nonviolent Communication: A Language of Life*. Encinitas, CA: Puddledancer Press, 2015.

Schaaf, Kathe; Kay Lindahl; Kathleen S. Hurty and Guo Cheen. *Women, Spirituality and Transformative Leadership: Where Grace Meets Power*. Woodstock, VT: SkyLight Paths Publishing, 2012.

Stein, Diane. *Casting the Circle: A Women's Book of Ritual*. Freedom, CA: The Crossing Press, 1990.

Steiner, Tej. *Heart Circles: How Sitting in Circle Can Transform Your World*. Phoenix, OR: Interactive Media Publishing, 2006.

Zimmerman, Jack. *The Way of Council*. Wilton Manors, FL: Bramble Books, 2009.

Acknowledgments

Thanks to Michael and Helena Cooper for their support on so many different levels!

I want to offer my boundless gratitude to all those who came to my circles and shared their beauty and wisdom with me. I hope my love, respect and admiration for each one of you shines through these pages.

About the Author

JALAJA BONHEIM, Ph.D. is one of the world's foremost experts in the use of circle gatherings as a tool for healing and empowering women. An inspiring visionary, internationally acclaimed speaker and award winning author, she mentors and trains women leaders worldwide. Founder of the Institute for Circlework, she has been leading circles for over three decades and has trained hundreds of Circlework leaders from around the world. She has gathered special acclaim for her groundbreaking work in the Middle East, where her circles unite Jewish and Palestinian women.

Jalaja Bonheim is the author of many books including *Aphrodite's Daughters: Women's Sexual Stories and the Journey of the Soul* and *The Sacred Ego: Making Peace with Ourselves and Our World,* which won the Nautilus Award for best book of 2015. To learn more about Jalaja Bonheim's work, including books, events and online courses, please visit www.jalajabonheim.com.

CPSIA information can be obtained
at www.ICGtesting.com
Printed in the USA
LVHW06s1523240818
587439LV00004B/217/P